I0837982

Victim Chic

Prologue

Prologue

The concept of victimhood is a pervasive one in modern society, and its influence can be seen in a wide range of contexts, from personal relationships to political systems. However, the ways in which individuals understand and respond to victimhood are not fixed or predetermined, but rather shaped by a complex interplay of individual and social factors. In this book, we have explored the impact of various factors on victimhood, including culture, trauma, identity, privilege, spirituality, politics, and education. By examining these factors in depth and providing strategies for cultivating a more empowering and transformative approach to adversity, this book has sought to challenge harmful narratives around victimhood and provide readers with the tools and resources necessary to move beyond victimhood and create meaningful change in their lives and communities.

1.Introduction: Defining Victim Chic and its Impact on Society

Victim chic is a cultural phenomenon that has gained significant attention in recent years due to its pervasive influence on contemporary culture. The concept of victim chic refers to the glorification of victimhood, where individuals adopt a victim identity as a means of gaining recognition and social status. Despite the historical association of victimhood with shame and disempowerment, in modern times, victimhood is often celebrated and viewed as a form of empowerment. The rise of victim chic can be attributed to various social and cultural factors, including the growing focus on individual rights and identity politics, as well as the influence of social media and celebrity culture. While victim chic may appear to offer benefits to individuals seeking recognition and validation, it can have negative consequences for both individuals and society, including a sense of entitlement, social divisions, and reduced empathy for others. Understanding the dynamics of victim chic is critical for developing strategies to address its negative impact and fostering a more nuanced understanding of victimhood in contemporary culture.

The term "victim chic" refers to the cultural phenomenon where individuals seek to gain social status or recognition by adopting a victim identity and glorifying victimhood. This trend has become increasingly prevalent in contemporary culture, where victimhood is often celebrated as a form of empowerment rather than seen as a state of disempowerment or suffering. Individuals who engage in victim chic often use their victim status as a means of gaining sympathy or attention from others, with the ultimate goal of elevating their social status. The negative consequences of victim chic include a sense of entitlement, social divisions, and reduced empathy for others. It is essential to understand the dynamics of victim chic and its impact on individuals and society to address this issue and foster a more nuanced understanding of victimhood.

While victimhood has historically been associated with shame and disempowerment, in contemporary culture it has become increasingly associated with empowerment and social status. In the past, victimhood was often associated with shame and disempowerment. However, in contemporary culture, there has been a shift towards seeing victimhood as a form of empowerment and social status. This shift has been fueled by the rise of identity politics, where individuals with marginalized identities have sought recognition and empowerment through their victim status. Additionally, the increasing influence of social media has enabled individuals to share their experiences of victimization more widely and gain recognition for their suffering. This new understanding of victimhood as empowering and socially desirable has given rise to the cultural phenomenon of victim chic. While this trend has brought attention to important issues of social justice, it also has negative consequences, such as a lack of empathy for others and the promotion of a victim mentality.

The rise of victim chic is driven by a variety of social and cultural factors, including the growing focus on individual rights and identity politics, as well as the influence of social media and celebrity culture. One of the primary drivers is the increasing focus on individual rights and identity politics, where individuals with marginalized identities seek recognition and empowerment through their victim status. This has led to a cultural shift where victimhood is often celebrated and viewed as a form of empowerment. Additionally, the influence of social media has allowed individuals to share their experiences of victimization with a wider audience, providing them with a platform to gain recognition for their suffering. Celebrity culture has also played a role, with celebrities often using their victim status to gain sympathy and social status. Overall, these cultural factors have contributed to the emergence of victim chic, which has both positive and negative consequences for society.

Despite its apparent benefits, victim chic can have negative consequences for both individuals and society as a whole, including fostering a culture of entitlement, exacerbating social divisions, and diminishing our ability to empathize with others.
While victim chic has its perceived benefits, it also has negative consequences that can be detrimental to individuals and society as a whole. By glorifying victimhood and the victim identity, it can foster a culture of entitlement where individuals feel entitled to recognition, sympathy, and special treatment. This can exacerbate social divisions, creating a sense of us versus them mentality that undermines the possibility of finding common ground and working towards solutions. Moreover,

victim chic can also diminish our ability to empathize with others, as it encourages individuals to view themselves as victims, rather than focusing on the commonalities that unite us. Overall, while victimhood is a real and important issue that should be addressed, the glorification of victimhood as a means of gaining social status is problematic and has negative consequences.

By exploring the dynamics of victim chic and its impact on individuals and society, we can better understand the cultural and psychological factors that contribute to its growth, and develop strategies for addressing its negative effects.
By examining victim chic and its effects on individuals and society, we can gain a deeper understanding of the cultural and psychological drivers that fuel its growth. This understanding can help us to develop strategies to mitigate its negative consequences, such as entitlement, social division, and lack of empathy. Moreover, understanding victim chic can help us to better support those who have experienced genuine trauma and to create a more compassionate and equitable society. In this book, we will explore the various dimensions of victim chic, from its cultural and political roots to its psychological and spiritual impact, and provide practical guidance for building resilience and developing a growth mindset in the face of adversity.

In this chapter, we will define victim chic, explore its historical roots and contemporary manifestations, and examine its impact on our social and political landscape.
In the first chapter, we will delve into the concept of victim chic and its impact on our society. We will begin by defining the term and exploring its historical roots, tracing its evolution from a symbol of disempowerment to a tool for social recognition and empowerment. We will then examine the contemporary manifestations of victim chic, including the ways in which it has infiltrated popular culture, social media, and politics. Finally, we will discuss the impact of victim chic on our social and political landscape, and explore how it has contributed to the polarization and fragmentation of our society. Through this exploration, we hope to gain a deeper understanding of victim chic and its effects, and develop strategies for addressing its negative consequences.

We will also consider the ways in which victim chic intersects with other social and cultural phenomena, such as cancel culture and identity politics, and discuss the implications of these intersections for our understanding of victimhood.
In addition to examining victim chic on its own, it is important to consider how it intersects with other social and cultural phenomena. One such phenomenon is cancel culture, which has been criticized for its reliance on victim narratives and the power dynamics it creates. Similarly, identity politics often relies on the recognition of group-based victimhood as a means of achieving political or social goals. By exploring these intersections, we can gain a more nuanced understanding of the role of victimhood in contemporary culture and the ways in which it shapes our collective identity.

By establishing a clear understanding of what victim chic is and its impact on society, we can lay the groundwork for a deeper exploration of its causes, consequences, and potential solutions. Victim chic is a complex and multifaceted phenomenon that requires a nuanced understanding. By defining victim chic and its impact on society in this chapter, we can begin to explore the psychological and cultural factors that contribute to its growth. With this foundation in place, we can delve into the intersections between victim chic and other social and cultural trends, such as identity politics and cancel culture. By doing so, we can develop a deeper understanding of the implications of victim chic for our social and political landscape. Ultimately, our aim is to foster a more empathetic and resilient society by addressing the negative effects of victim chic and promoting a more constructive approach to overcoming adversity.

Ultimately, our goal is to develop a more nuanced and critical understanding of victimhood and its role in shaping our individual and collective identities.
Our ultimate goal in examining victim chic is to move beyond simplistic and polarized understandings of victimhood, and to develop a more nuanced and critical perspective on the role it plays in shaping our individual and collective identities. By interrogating the cultural and psychological factors that drive the phenomenon of victim chic, we can better understand its impact on society and explore strategies for promoting a healthier and more productive relationship with victimhood. Through this process, we can develop a deeper appreciation for the complexity and diversity of human experiences and perspectives, and build a more compassionate and inclusive society.

2. The Psychology of Victimhood: Understanding Why People Identify as Victims

•

Victimhood can be defined as the experience of having been harmed, oppressed, or mistreated in some way. This experience can take many forms, ranging from physical violence to emotional abuse, and can result in a range of negative outcomes, including trauma, anxiety, and depression. While victimhood is a universal experience that has been present throughout human history, it is also a culturally constructed concept that varies across different societies and time periods. Understanding the nature of victimhood, and the ways in which it is constructed and experienced, is essential for developing effective strategies for supporting victims and promoting healing and recovery.

However, victimhood is not just a passive state of being, but can also involve active strategies for coping with and responding to adversity. Victimhood is often associated with a sense of powerlessness and passivity, but it is important to recognize that individuals who experience victimization may also engage in active coping strategies to address their experiences of harm or oppression. These strategies can include seeking support from others, taking legal action, or engaging in advocacy or activism. In this way, victimhood is not simply a state of being, but also a set of actions and responses that individuals may use to navigate their experiences of adversity. Recognizing this complexity is important for understanding the varied experiences of victims and for developing effective interventions and supports to help individuals recover from traumatic experiences.

Victimhood can be experienced on multiple levels, including individual, group, and societal. At the individual level, victimhood may involve experiences of personal trauma, such as physical or emotional abuse, neglect, or other forms of mistreatment. Group victimhood, on the other hand, refers to the collective experiences of a particular social or cultural group, such as racism, sexism, or homophobia. Societal victimhood involves broader issues of power and inequality, such as economic exploitation or political oppression. Each level of victimhood is interconnected and can impact one another, and understanding these connections is important for developing effective strategies for coping with and addressing victimization.

The experience of victimhood is complex and can vary widely depending on a range of factors, including culture, gender, race, and socioeconomic status. For instance, individuals from marginalized communities may be more likely to experience victimization due to *perceived* systemic oppression and discrimination, while those from privileged backgrounds may be more likely to experience victimization due to individual or interpersonal conflicts. Additionally, the cultural and social expectations surrounding victimhood may differ across communities, with some emphasizing resilience and self-reliance and others emphasizing solidarity and collective action. Understanding these diverse experiences of victimhood is essential for developing effective interventions and supporting those who have been harmed.

Victimhood can be seen as a social construct that is shaped by broader cultural and political trends. In many societies, victimhood has been stigmatized and associated with weakness, shame, and even moral culpability. However, in contemporary culture, victimhood is increasingly celebrated as a means of gaining social recognition and legitimacy. This shift can be attributed to a variety of factors, including the growing emphasis on individual rights, the influence of identity politics, and the impact of social media and other forms of digital communication. By examining the social and cultural context in which victimhood arises, we can gain a better understanding of its meaning and significance for individuals and society.

The experience of victimhood is dynamic and complex, influenced by a range of internal and external factors. Individuals may feel victimized in response to a variety of life experiences, such as personal trauma, discrimination, or economic hardship. The experience of victimhood can also be shaped by social and cultural narratives that define who is considered a victim and what types of experiences are seen as legitimate. Moreover, the experience of victimhood can evolve over time, as individuals may move from a state of feeling victimized to one of resilience and empowerment. Understanding the multidimensional nature of victimhood is essential for developing effective strategies for supporting individuals who have experienced adversity.

Understanding the dynamics of victimhood is crucial for promoting empathy, social justice, and resilience in individuals and communities. By recognizing the diverse ways in which people experience victimization and the complex social and cultural factors that contribute to these experiences, we can better support individuals who have experienced harm and work to address the root causes of victimization. Additionally, by developing a nuanced understanding of victimhood, we can foster greater empathy and understanding among individuals and communities, and work towards creating a more just and equitable society for all.

Research on victimhood has been a topic of interest across various fields, including psychology, sociology, and political science. Scholars have examined the role of victimhood in shaping individual and group identities, as well as its impact on social and political outcomes. Studies have explored the psychological and emotional consequences of victimization, such as trauma, post-traumatic stress disorder (PTSD), and depression. In addition, researchers have investigated the ways in which victimhood is constructed and perpetuated through social and political processes, including the media, public discourse, and policy-making. By drawing on insights from multiple disciplines, we can develop a more comprehensive understanding of victimhood and its impact on society.

Some scholars have argued that not all claims of victimhood are equal, and have proposed a distinction between "authentic" and "malignant" victimhood. Authentic victimhood refers to situations in which individuals or groups have experienced real harm or injustice, and their claims to victim status are seen as legitimate. Malignant victimhood, on the other hand, refers to situations in which individuals or groups adopt a victim identity for strategic or manipulative purposes, and their claims to victim status are seen as illegitimate. This distinction can help us to better understand the complexities of victimhood, and to identify situations in which claims of victimhood may be more or less deserving of recognition and support.

The idea of victimhood is often the subject of political debate and controversy. In many cases, claims to victimhood are used to support various policy positions, such as affirmative action, immigration reform, or criminal justice reform. Some argue that certain groups are unfairly labeled as victims and use their perceived victim status to gain advantages or special treatment. Understanding the complexities of victimhood is crucial for engaging in constructive dialogues and promoting social justice.

Critiques of victimhood have gained traction in recent years, with some scholars arguing that it can be used to justify harmful or counterproductive behaviors. For example, some have suggested that the adoption of a victim mentality can lead individuals to feel entitled to special treatment or exempt from personal responsibility. Additionally, some argue that the glorification of victimhood can create a culture of blame and resentment, rather than one of resilience and empowerment. These critiques highlight the need for a more nuanced and balanced understanding of victimhood, one that acknowledges the real experiences of harm and injustice while also recognizing the potential pitfalls of excessive victimization.

Victimhood intersects with a range of social identities and experiences, including race, gender, and class. For instance, individuals who belong to marginalized racial or ethnic groups may experience victimhood as a result of systemic discrimination or violence. Similarly, women and members of the LGBTQ+ community may experience victimization as a result of gender-based violence or discrimination. Moreover, individuals from lower socioeconomic backgrounds may experience victimization as a result of economic exploitation or systemic inequality. Understanding these intersections is essential for developing a comprehensive understanding of victimhood and its impact on individuals and society.

3. Cultural Influences on Victimhood

Culture plays a significant role in shaping how individuals understand and experience victimhood. Cultural factors, such as values, beliefs, and social norms, can influence how people perceive and respond to adversity, as well as the degree to which they identify as victims. For example, some cultures may prioritize resilience and self-reliance, viewing victimhood as a sign of weakness, while others may value collectivism and emphasize the importance of support and solidarity with those who have been victimized. Understanding how cultural factors influence attitudes towards victimhood is crucial for promoting a healthy and balanced understanding of the phenomenon, and for encouraging individuals to take an active and empowered approach to adversity.

Cultural values, beliefs, and norms play a crucial role in shaping an individual's perception of victimhood and their response to victimization. For instance, in some cultures, seeking help and support for victimization is viewed as a sign of weakness, while in others, it is seen as a sign of strength. Additionally, cultural values surrounding individualism versus collectivism can affect how victims seek help and support. In individualistic cultures, victims may be encouraged to take matters into their own hands and seek individual justice, while in collectivist cultures, victims may seek support from their community and prioritize group harmony over individual justice. Understanding the influence of cultural values on victimhood can help to promote more effective responses to victimization and reduce negative outcomes associated with victimization.

In individualistic cultures, there is often a strong emphasis on self-reliance and personal responsibility. This can shape how individuals perceive themselves in relation to victimhood, with a decreased emphasis on victimhood and a focus on resilience and individual agency. In these cultures, individuals may be more likely to attribute their successes and failures to their own actions rather than external circumstances. While this can lead to a sense of empowerment and self-efficacy, it may also lead to a lack of understanding or empathy for those who have experienced victimization.

In contrast to individualistic cultures, collectivistic cultures tend to place a greater emphasis on the importance of group identity and social cohesion. As such, victimhood may take on a more prominent role in these societies as a means of securing social support and solidarity. In collectivistic cultures, individuals may be more likely to see themselves as part of a larger group or community, and may view harm to one member of the group as harm to the group as a whole. This can lead to a greater emphasis on victimhood as a means of mobilizing support and promoting social justice. However, it is important to note that not all individuals in collectivistic cultures will necessarily embrace victimhood as a central part of their identity or approach to adversity.

In societies where power and authority are highly valued, individuals with less power may be more likely to accept victimization as a result of the cultural emphasis on hierarchy and status. This can lead to a normalization of victimhood and a decreased emphasis on agency and personal responsibility. Conversely, societies that prioritize equality and social justice may be more likely to encourage individuals to resist victimization and take action to assert their rights and agency. Understanding the cultural values that shape attitudes towards victimhood can provide insight into how individuals and communities respond to victimization and can inform efforts to promote resilience and empowerment.

Religion and spirituality can have a significant influence on how individuals perceive victimhood. Some religions place a high value on suffering and sacrifice, viewing it as a means of spiritual growth or as a path to moral purity. This can lead to a greater acceptance of victimhood as a way of demonstrating faithfulness or piety. However, other religious traditions may place a greater emphasis on personal responsibility and agency, discouraging individuals from identifying as victims and instead focusing on resilience and self-improvement. Cultural and historical factors can also influence religious attitudes towards victimhood, with some societies venerating figures who have suffered oppression or persecution as a means of promoting social justice and solidarity.

The media can influence cultural attitudes towards victimhood by shaping how individuals perceive and respond to victimization. While media coverage can draw attention to important issues and raise awareness of social injustices, it can also perpetuate a victim mentality that encourages individuals to see themselves as powerless and reliant on external sources for validation and support. The media may also create a competitive culture of victimhood, where individuals or groups seek to outdo each other in their claims of victimization. This can lead to a culture where victimhood is perceived as a desirable status, rather than an unfortunate circumstance to be overcome. Therefore, it is important to critically evaluate media messages and promote a more balanced and constructive understanding of victimhood.

Historical events and collective memories can have a lasting impact on cultural attitudes towards victimhood. Past traumas and injustices, such as genocide, slavery, or colonization, can create a collective consciousness of victimization that extends across generations. Such events may lead to a heightened sensitivity to victimization, as well as a greater emphasis on collective healing and social justice. At the same time, historical victimhood can also become a source of identity and political mobilization, as groups seek recognition, reparations, or social change in response to past harm. The way in which societies come to terms with historical trauma can have significant implications for how individuals perceive and respond to victimhood in the present day.

Cultural attitudes towards mental health and well-being can have a significant impact on how individuals perceive and cope with victimization. Societies that stigmatize mental illness may be less likely to acknowledge or seek help for emotional distress related to victimization, leading to a decreased emphasis on victimhood and a focus on coping mechanisms such as avoidance or stoicism. Conversely, societies that prioritize mental health may encourage individuals to seek support and share their experiences of victimization, potentially increasing the importance of victimhood as a means of promoting healing and resilience.

In Mark Manson's book, "The Subtle Art of Not Giving a Fuck," he discusses how cultural attitudes towards masculinity and femininity can impact perceptions of victimhood. In some societies, traditional notions of masculinity may equate victimhood with weakness or vulnerability, leading individuals to avoid identifying as a victim and to prioritize self-reliance and toughness. On the other hand, societies that place greater emphasis on empathy and compassion may view victimhood as a valid and important experience, regardless of gender. Manson argues that these cultural attitudes can be problematic, perpetuating harmful stereotypes and preventing individuals from seeking the support they need in the aftermath of victimization. He encourages readers to challenge these attitudes and to view vulnerability and empathy as strengths, rather than weaknesses.

In Mark Manson's book, "The Subtle Art of Not Giving a Fuck," the concept of victim chic in popular culture is explored. The book argues that victimhood has become a status symbol, particularly in Western societies, where it is often glamorized and rewarded. This is reflected in popular culture, with movies and TV shows frequently portraying characters who have overcome adversity and emerged as victorious victims. The book suggests that this cultural narrative can encourage individuals to adopt a victim mentality as a means of gaining attention and validation, rather than focusing on personal growth and resilience. By understanding the influence of popular culture on attitudes towards victimhood, individuals can become more conscious of the narratives they consume and how they may impact their own beliefs and behaviors.

The use of humor and satire in relation to victimhood is a complex and often contentious issue. Some cultures view humor as a means of coping with difficult situations and may use it to make light of their own victimization or to highlight the absurdity of certain situations. However, others may see this type of humor as insensitive or even offensive, particularly if it is used to trivialize the experiences of victims or to reinforce harmful stereotypes. Satire, in particular, can be a powerful tool for critiquing social norms and challenging the status quo, but it can also be misinterpreted or co-opted for other purposes. Understanding the cultural attitudes towards humor and satire in relation to victimhood is important for recognizing the potential impact of these forms of expression on victims and the wider society.

Cultural factors are not experienced in a vacuum and can intersect with other social identities and experiences. For example, in some cultures, being a victim may be seen as a sign of weakness or a failure to take personal responsibility, and this attitude may be amplified for individuals who are members of marginalized groups. This can lead to a dismissal or minimization of their experiences of victimization. On the other hand, cultures that prioritize empathy and compassion may be more likely to acknowledge and validate the experiences of victims, particularly for individuals from historically marginalized communities. The intersection of cultural factors with other social identities and experiences adds complexity to our understanding of victimhood and highlights the need for a nuanced approach to addressing and responding to victimization.

Cultural influences on victimhood can have a significant impact on how individuals perceive and respond to victimization. However, the impact of cultural factors can vary widely depending on the individual and the specific context. For example, individuals from collectivistic cultures may place a greater emphasis on victimhood as a means of securing social support and solidarity, while individuals from individualistic cultures may prioritize resilience and personal agency over victimhood. It is also important to consider how cultural attitudes intersect with other social identities and experiences, such as race, gender, and sexuality, which can further shape perceptions of victimhood. Ultimately, a nuanced and culturally sensitive approach is necessary to better understand and respond to the complex and multifaceted phenomenon of victimhood.

Understanding the cultural influences on victimhood is critical for developing effective strategies to support individuals who have experienced victimization. By recognizing how cultural attitudes and values shape perceptions of victimhood, individuals and communities can develop culturally sensitive approaches to promoting resilience and healing. Furthermore, understanding the intersection of cultural influences with other social identities and experiences can help develop comprehensive approaches to addressing systemic inequalities and promoting social justice. By acknowledging and addressing the cultural factors that influence victimhood, individuals and communities can work towards creating a more supportive and equitable society for all.

4. Discouraging Victimhood

Encouraging personal responsibility and self-reflection is crucial for promoting growth and development in individuals. Externalizing blame for one's problems can lead to a victim mentality, where individuals feel helpless and powerless in their circumstances. Instead, promoting personal responsibility and self-reflection can empower individuals to take ownership of their lives and make positive changes. It requires acknowledging one's mistakes and taking steps to address them, rather than blaming others or circumstances for one's challenges. By developing a sense of personal agency, individuals can cultivate resilience and adaptability, which are essential for overcoming adversity and achieving success in life.

Encouraging a growth mindset can be a powerful way to help individuals overcome victim mentality and develop a sense of personal agency. By emphasizing the belief that one can learn and improve, rather than being limited by fixed traits or circumstances, individuals can begin to see their challenges as opportunities for growth and development. This can lead to increased motivation, resilience, and a greater willingness to take on challenges and pursue goals. Emphasizing the importance of effort and hard work, rather than innate talent or ability, can also help individuals develop a stronger sense of self-efficacy and confidence in their ability to succeed. Ultimately, cultivating a growth mindset can be a valuable tool for empowering individuals to take control of their lives and achieve their goals.

Promoting a culture of resilience is essential for combating victim chic and creating a society that values personal agency and empowerment. Rather than emphasizing fragility or victimhood, resilience focuses on building coping skills and emotional strength to navigate challenges and overcome adversity. Encouraging individuals to develop resilience requires providing opportunities for learning and growth, emphasizing the importance of self-care and mindfulness practices, and promoting a growth mindset that emphasizes the ability to learn and improve. This can involve providing resources for therapy or counseling, promoting physical health and exercise, and creating supportive communities where individuals can find connection and support. By promoting resilience, we can help individuals cultivate the strength and adaptability they need to thrive in the face of life's challenges.

Encouraging a sense of agency and empowerment is essential in promoting resilience and overcoming victim chic. This involves shifting the focus from external factors to internal ones, emphasizing personal responsibility and the ability to make choices and take action. By recognizing that we have agency in our lives, we can take ownership of our circumstances and work towards achieving our goals. This can involve setting realistic goals, breaking down larger tasks into smaller ones, and developing a plan of action to achieve them. It also involves acknowledging and learning from mistakes and failures, and using them as opportunities for growth and self-improvement. Ultimately, fostering a sense of agency and empowerment can lead to greater self-confidence, motivation, and success in all areas of life.

Fostering a sense of community and social connection is essential in promoting resilience and well-being. Having a strong social support network can help individuals cope with adversity and overcome challenges. It provides a sense of belonging and security, which can reduce stress and anxiety. Encouraging social connections and building relationships can also lead to increased empathy and understanding, creating a more compassionate and supportive community. Additionally, being part of a community can provide opportunities for personal growth and development, such as learning new skills, trying new experiences, and engaging in meaningful activities with others. By emphasizing the importance of social connection, we can promote a culture of resilience and help individuals thrive.

Encouraging a focus on strengths and positive qualities can be a powerful tool for promoting resilience and well-being. By emphasizing what individuals are capable of rather than what they lack, they can develop a sense of agency and self-efficacy. This can help individuals to feel more confident in their abilities to navigate challenges and overcome obstacles, leading to a greater sense of empowerment and a more positive outlook on life. Additionally, focusing on strengths can help to cultivate a sense of self-worth and purpose, as individuals recognize their unique talents and contributions to the world around them.

On the other hand, when individuals focus primarily on their deficits and limitations, it can lead to feelings of helplessness and a sense of being trapped by circumstances. This can create a cycle of negative thinking that reinforces a victim mentality, making it difficult to break free and move forward. By shifting the focus to strengths and positive qualities, individuals can break out of this cycle and begin to see their potential for growth and change. Encouraging this shift in perspective can be a powerful tool for promoting personal agency and resilience, helping individuals to overcome adversity and thrive in their lives.

Promoting a culture of gratitude and appreciation can have a powerful impact on one's well-being and resilience. Focusing on the positive aspects of life can help individuals develop a more optimistic and hopeful outlook, which in turn can lead to greater resilience in the face of adversity. Research has shown that regularly practicing gratitude can increase happiness, reduce stress and anxiety, and even improve physical health. Encouraging individuals to take time to reflect on the things they are grateful for can help shift their focus away from negative experiences and cultivate a sense of appreciation for the good things in life, no matter how small they may be.

Encouraging the development of realistic and achievable goals is crucial for promoting resilience and success. When individuals have a clear sense of what they want to achieve and a plan for how to get there, they are more likely to be motivated and persistent in their efforts. It is important to emphasize the importance of effort and persistence in achieving success, as setbacks and challenges are inevitable along the way. By acknowledging these challenges and focusing on the effort required to overcome them, individuals can develop a sense of agency and control over their lives. Additionally, it is important to ensure that goals are realistic and achievable, as setting overly ambitious or unrealistic goals can lead to frustration and disappointment. By setting achievable goals and celebrating incremental progress, individuals can build confidence and a sense of accomplishment, which can fuel further success.

Promoting a sense of personal accountability is an important aspect of fostering resilience and promoting personal growth. Encouraging individuals to take responsibility for their actions and choices can help them feel empowered and in control of their lives. It also helps individuals to learn from their mistakes and make positive changes in their behavior. By taking ownership of their actions, individuals can develop a stronger sense of self-awareness and make intentional choices that align with their values and goals. Encouraging personal accountability can also help individuals to overcome feelings of helplessness or victimhood by focusing on what they can do rather than what is outside of their control. Overall, promoting personal accountability can lead to greater self-esteem, motivation, and a sense of purpose in life.

Encouraging the development of a growth mindset is essential for promoting personal growth and resilience. A growth mindset is the belief that one's abilities and qualities can be developed and improved through effort and learning. This perspective emphasizes the importance of continuous learning and effort in achieving success, rather than being limited by fixed traits or circumstances. Individuals with a growth mindset are more likely to persist in the face of challenges, view failures as opportunities for growth, and take risks to pursue their goals. Encouraging a growth mindset can lead to increased confidence and motivation, and help individuals to better cope with setbacks and adversity. By fostering a culture of growth and development, individuals can achieve their full potential and create meaningful lives.

Adopting a victim identity as a means of gaining social status or recognition can be harmful to both the individual and society as a whole. By focusing solely on one's struggles and hardships, individuals may neglect their personal strengths and abilities, leading to a sense of powerlessness and helplessness. This can also perpetuate a cycle of blame and resentment, hindering personal growth and hindering the development of healthy relationships with others. Moreover, it can lead to a culture of victimhood, where individuals are encouraged to prioritize their perceived victim status over personal responsibility and accountability. As such, it is important to discourage the adoption of a victim identity and instead promote a culture of resilience and personal agency.

The glorification of victimhood in popular culture and media can lead to the adoption of a victim identity as a means of gaining social status or recognition. This can be harmful as it reinforces a sense of powerlessness and discourages personal responsibility and self-reliance. It is important to challenge this narrative and promote a culture of resilience and empowerment. By emphasizing the importance of personal agency and the ability to learn and grow from adversity, we can encourage individuals to take ownership of their lives and work towards creating positive change. Additionally, promoting positive role models and examples of resilience in popular media can help shift the cultural narrative away from victimhood and towards strength and adaptability.

Promoting critical thinking and skepticism is important in countering the proliferation of victimhood narratives. Encouraging individuals to question assumptions and think critically about the messages they receive in the media and from other sources can help them to recognize and reject narratives that promote victimhood as a means of gaining power or attention. This can include questioning the validity of statistics or stories that are presented without evidence, as well as examining the motivations of those who are promoting a particular narrative. By fostering critical thinking and skepticism, individuals can become more aware of the ways in which victimhood narratives can be used to manipulate and control others, and can begin to develop more nuanced and complex understandings of the world around them. This can ultimately lead to a greater sense of personal agency and resilience, as individuals become better equipped to navigate the challenges and complexities of their lives.

Encouraging a focus on solutions and problem-solving is an important aspect of promoting personal agency and resilience. Rather than dwelling on problems and grievances, individuals can benefit from identifying and pursuing actionable steps towards addressing challenges and achieving their goals. This approach involves a shift from a passive, victim mentality to an active, problem-solving mentality. By adopting a proactive mindset, individuals can feel more in control of their lives and empowered to take action towards positive change. This can involve developing effective problem-solving skills, seeking out resources and support, and adopting a growth mindset that emphasizes learning and growth from setbacks. By promoting a focus on solutions and problem-solving, individuals can cultivate a sense of personal agency and resilience that can help them overcome challenges and achieve their goals.

Developing coping skills and emotional regulation can be critical in promoting resilience and adaptability in the face of adversity. Individuals who are able to effectively cope with stressors and regulate their emotions are better equipped to handle difficult situations and bounce back from setbacks. Coping skills can take many forms, including mindfulness meditation, exercise, journaling, or talking with a trusted friend or counselor. By engaging in these activities, individuals can learn to manage their emotions and maintain a sense of calm in the face of challenges. Additionally, by developing resilience and adaptability, individuals can build confidence in their ability to handle whatever life may throw their way. This can promote a sense of personal agency and empowerment, enabling individuals to take control of their lives and pursue their goals with confidence.

It is important to challenge the belief that one's identity or group membership necessarily defines one's experience of victimization. While systemic discrimination and oppression based on race, gender, sexual orientation, and other factors undoubtedly exist, it is also true that individuals within these groups may have vastly different experiences based on a variety of factors such as personal circumstances, social support, and individual agency. It is important to recognize and respect the unique experiences of individuals while also acknowledging the complexity and nuance of the ways in which identity intersects with experiences of victimization. By challenging simplistic and reductive narratives that essentialize identity, we can create space for a more nuanced and inclusive understanding of the experiences of individuals who have faced adversity.

Encouraging a sense of personal agency and control is essential for promoting resilience and overcoming victim chic. When individuals believe that they have control over their lives and the ability to make choices that can positively impact their future, they are more likely to feel empowered and take action towards achieving their goals. This sense of agency can be fostered by emphasizing the importance of taking responsibility for one's own life and decisions, rather than externalizing blame or attributing success or failure solely to external factors. Encouraging individuals to identify and pursue their personal goals and passions can also promote a sense of agency and control, as they are able to shape their lives around what matters most to them. Ultimately, promoting personal agency can help individuals develop the skills and mindset needed to overcome challenges and navigate adversity with resilience and perseverance.

Promoting a growth mindset is crucial in fostering resilience and personal growth. Instead of being limited by fixed traits or circumstances, a growth mindset emphasizes the ability to learn, adapt, and improve. Individuals who cultivate a growth mindset believe that their abilities and talents can be developed through hard work, practice, and learning from mistakes. This mindset encourages individuals to take on challenges, persevere through obstacles, and view failures as opportunities for growth. By embracing a growth mindset, individuals can develop a sense of agency and control over their lives, as well as a willingness to take risks and pursue their goals. In promoting a growth mindset, we can encourage individuals to unlock their full potential and cultivate a sense of resilience and adaptability in the face of adversity.

It is important to challenge the belief that victimhood is a fixed or permanent state of being. While experiencing trauma and adversity can be extremely difficult, it is important to recognize that it does not have to define one's entire life. Encouraging a growth mindset can be a powerful tool in promoting resilience and empowering individuals to overcome their challenges. By emphasizing the ability to learn and improve, individuals can begin to see their struggles as opportunities for growth and change rather than insurmountable obstacles. It is important to emphasize that the journey towards healing and growth may be difficult, but it is possible with time, effort, and a willingness to embrace the potential for change. By promoting the belief that growth and change are possible, individuals can move beyond a fixed victim identity and embrace a more empowered and resilient sense of self.

Encouraging a focus on personal strengths and positive qualities is essential in promoting resilience and well-being. Instead of dwelling on weaknesses or shortcomings, individuals can benefit greatly from identifying and building on their existing assets. This approach can provide a sense of empowerment and agency, as well as a foundation for achieving personal goals. By acknowledging and leveraging their strengths, individuals can develop a greater sense of self-confidence and self-efficacy, which in turn can help them navigate challenges and setbacks with greater resilience. This focus on strengths can also promote positive emotions and a sense of fulfillment, contributing to overall well-being and life satisfaction. Therefore, it is crucial to encourage individuals to identify and cultivate their personal strengths, rather than focusing solely on areas of perceived deficiency.

Finding purpose and meaning in life is essential for promoting resilience and well-being. When individuals have a clear sense of what is important to them, they are better able to navigate the challenges and setbacks that may arise. Encouraging the development of a sense of purpose and meaning can be done in various ways, such as helping individuals identify their passions and values, providing opportunities for volunteerism or service, or helping individuals find meaning in their work or relationships. By promoting a sense of purpose and meaning, individuals are better equipped to find fulfillment in their lives, even in the face of adversity. This can help promote a sense of resilience and enable individuals to bounce back from setbacks with renewed energy and determination.

5. The Dangers of Victim Mentality: How it Limits Personal Growth and Success

Victim mentality is a state of mind that is characterized by a persistent belief in being powerless to change one's circumstances. Individuals with a victim mentality often view themselves as being at the mercy of external forces, such as other people, the environment, or their own past experiences. They may feel overwhelmed by life's challenges and struggle to take action to improve their situation. In some cases, individuals with a victim mentality may even actively seek out situations that reinforce their sense of helplessness or victimhood, such as seeking out sympathy or attention from others. This can lead to a cycle of negative thinking and behavior that reinforces their belief in their powerlessness and makes it difficult to break free from the victim mentality. It is important to recognize the potential harm of victim mentality and work towards cultivating a more empowered and resilient mindset.

A victim mentality can be limiting, as it can prevent individuals from taking responsibility for their own lives and making meaningful change. Believing that one is powerless and at the mercy of external circumstances can create a sense of hopelessness and discourage individuals from seeking out opportunities for growth and development. This mentality can also reinforce a sense of dependence on others, as individuals may feel that they are unable to make meaningful changes on their own. As a result, it is important to challenge the victim mentality and encourage individuals to take ownership of their lives, recognizing that they have the power to shape their own destinies. By doing so, individuals can cultivate a sense of agency and empowerment, which can promote personal growth, resilience, and well-being.

People with a victim mentality may be inclined to blame others for their problems, rather than taking responsibility for their own actions and choices. This can limit their ability to make meaningful changes in their lives and can perpetuate a cycle of victimhood. Focusing on external factors that they perceive as causing their problems can also prevent individuals from developing a sense of agency and empowerment, which are essential for personal growth and development. Encouraging individuals to take responsibility for their actions and choices, and to focus on solutions rather than problems, can help them develop a more resilient and proactive mindset. By doing so, they can build the skills and confidence needed to navigate challenges and create a more fulfilling life.

Victim mentality can be detrimental to an individual's overall well-being and sense of agency. Those who adopt this mentality may feel as though their circumstances are out of their control, leading to a sense of helplessness and despair. This can be particularly damaging as it may lead to a lack of motivation to take action to improve one's situation. Instead, individuals with a victim mentality may feel as though their fate is determined by external factors, such as societal norms or the actions of others. This can result in feelings of frustration, anger, and resentment, further perpetuating the cycle of victimhood. Overall, it is important to encourage a sense of personal agency and empowerment in order to break free from the limitations of victim mentality and move towards a more fulfilling and purposeful life.

Chronic victimhood can have detrimental effects on an individual's sense of self-worth and self-esteem. The persistent belief in being powerless and helpless can contribute to a negative self-image, leading to feelings of unworthiness or incompetence. This negative self-perception can become a self-fulfilling prophecy, as the individual may begin to doubt their abilities and limit their opportunities for growth and success. In addition, chronic victimhood can lead to a sense of resentment towards others and the world, resulting in a lack of trust and difficulty forming meaningful relationships. It is important to challenge and overcome a victim mentality in order to cultivate a positive self-image and achieve personal growth and fulfillment.

Victims may develop a sense of entitlement due to their perception of being unfairly treated or mistreated. This can lead to the belief that others owe them something or that others should fix their problems. This expectation of external help can result in a lack of personal responsibility and accountability. When individuals adopt a victim mentality, they may become passive and disengaged from their own lives, waiting for someone else to take charge. This can lead to a lack of motivation and initiative, which can be detrimental to personal growth and development. It is important to encourage individuals to take ownership of their lives and to be proactive in finding solutions to their problems, rather than relying on others to solve their problems for them.

The victim mentality can have a profound impact on an individual's social relationships, leading to feelings of isolation and disconnection. People with a victim mentality may believe that others do not understand or empathize with their experiences, leading to a sense of alienation and social withdrawal. Additionally, the belief that one is constantly being victimized can lead to a tendency to view others with suspicion and mistrust, further isolating the individual from potential sources of support and connection. Over time, these patterns can contribute to a sense of loneliness and social disconnection, which can further reinforce the victim mentality and make it difficult to break free from its grip.

When individuals adopt a victim mentality, they may become trapped in a self-perpetuating cycle that reinforces their sense of powerlessness and victimization. This can occur when individuals repeatedly seek out and identify with victim narratives, which can further solidify their beliefs that they are helpless to change their circumstances. As a result, individuals may become resistant to alternative perspectives or solutions, making it difficult for them to break free from the cycle of victimhood. In order to break this cycle, it is important for individuals to take responsibility for their own actions and choices, and to actively seek out opportunities for growth and personal development.

A victim mentality can be detrimental to one's mental and emotional well-being by reducing resilience and increasing vulnerability to stress. This can lead to an inability to cope with challenges and setbacks, resulting in feelings of hopelessness and helplessness. Individuals with a victim mentality may struggle to adapt to changing circumstances or overcome obstacles, as they may feel that their circumstances are out of their control. This can further reinforce a sense of powerlessness and contribute to a negative cycle of victimization. Developing a growth mindset and building resilience through coping skills and emotional regulation can help individuals break free from a victim mentality and develop a more positive and empowering outlook on life.

Individuals with a victim mentality may struggle with decision-making and problem-solving because they may feel that they lack control over their circumstances. This can lead to a sense of overwhelm and a belief that any actions taken will not make a difference in the outcome. As a result, they may become indecisive or rely on others to make decisions for them. Additionally, they may struggle to see potential solutions to problems and instead focus on external factors that are causing their difficulties. Developing a growth mindset and a sense of personal agency can be helpful in overcoming these challenges and building the skills needed for effective decision-making and problem-solving.

A victim mentality can also lead to a lack of motivation and a sense of hopelessness, as individuals may feel that their efforts will not make a difference in the face of their perceived victimization. This can result in a lack of ambition and a resignation to their circumstances, hindering personal growth and development. In addition, a victim mentality may contribute to a self-fulfilling prophecy, where individuals do not take action to improve their situation because they believe that their efforts will be futile. Encouraging individuals to focus on personal strengths and assets, and promoting a growth mindset, can help to combat the negative effects of a victim mentality and empower individuals to take control of their lives.

The victim mentality can create a sense of victimization and unfairness in individuals, leading to negative attitudes towards others and a lack of trust in society and institutions. People with this mindset may feel that the world is against them, and as a result, they may develop a cynical and pessimistic outlook on life. They may also struggle to form meaningful connections with others, as they may view relationships as a potential source of further victimization. Over time, this can lead to a sense of social isolation and further reinforce their victim identity. Ultimately, it is essential to challenge the victim mentality and promote a sense of personal agency and empowerment, as this is crucial for personal growth and well-being.

Victim mentality can sometimes lead to a sense of entitlement, where individuals feel that they are owed compensation or special treatment by society or other individuals. This sense of entitlement can create an unproductive and unhealthy dynamic, as individuals may become focused on what they believe they are owed rather than taking responsibility for their own actions and choices. Additionally, this entitlement mindset can foster resentment towards others who do not offer them what they feel they deserve, leading to further feelings of victimization and disconnection from others. It's important to encourage individuals to take ownership of their own lives and work towards their goals, rather than expecting handouts or special treatment based on a sense of victimization.

Individuals with a victim mentality may struggle to form healthy relationships due to their negative self-image and lack of personal responsibility. This mindset can create barriers to intimacy and emotional connection, as individuals may feel that they are not worthy of love or that others are responsible for their happiness. They may also struggle to communicate effectively and assert their needs, as they may believe that others should already know what they need and want. As a result, relationships with friends, family, and romantic partners may suffer, leading to further feelings of isolation and victimization.

The victim mentality can sometimes lead to a sense of moral superiority, as individuals may feel that their experiences of suffering and victimization give them a unique moral authority. This can result in a tendency to judge and condemn others who do not share the same experiences or perspectives, as well as a reluctance to consider alternative viewpoints or engage in constructive dialogue. In extreme cases, this can lead to a form of tribalism, where individuals identify primarily with their victimized group and view members of other groups with suspicion or hostility. It is important to recognize that while experiences of victimization can be profound and valid, they do not necessarily confer moral superiority or the right to impose one's views on others.

Individuals with a victim mentality may struggle to empathize with others, as they may view their own suffering as more significant or deserving of attention. This lack of empathy can create barriers to building healthy relationships and may contribute to a sense of social disconnection. Moreover, individuals with a victim mentality may be quick to judge others for not understanding their experiences, without recognizing the perspectives and challenges of others. This can lead to a lack of understanding and mutual respect, further perpetuating the cycle of victimhood.

Individuals with a victim mentality may find it challenging to forgive themselves or others, as they may believe that they have been unfairly treated and that forgiveness would imply accepting their victimization. This can lead to a perpetuation of negative emotions such as anger, resentment, and bitterness, which can further contribute to their victim mentality. It is important for individuals to recognize that forgiveness is a choice and that it does not necessarily mean condoning or forgetting the past. By choosing to forgive, individuals can free themselves from the burden of negative emotions and move towards a healthier and more positive outlook on life.

The victim mentality can be a self-fulfilling prophecy, leading to a sense of hopelessness and despair. When individuals believe that their circumstances are fixed and unchangeable, they may lose the motivation to take action and make positive changes in their lives. This can lead to feelings of helplessness and resignation, which can further reinforce the belief in victimhood. As a result, it can be challenging to break free from this cycle of negative thinking and regain a sense of agency and control over one's life. It is essential to challenge the belief that victimhood is a permanent state of being and to foster a growth mindset focused on personal empowerment and growth.

When an individual adopts a victim mentality, they often feel powerless to change their circumstances, leading to a negative self-image and a lack of personal responsibility. This can make it challenging for them to prioritize their own self-care and self-compassion. They may struggle with setting healthy boundaries or taking time for self-care activities because they feel guilty or believe that their problems are too significant to take a break. Additionally, individuals with a victim mentality may struggle with self-compassion, as they may view self-compassion as a weakness or believe that they do not deserve kindness and understanding. As a result, self-care and self-compassion may become challenging for individuals with a victim mentality, making it essential to break this cycle and promote a more growth-oriented mindset.

The victim mentality can be a vicious cycle that is difficult to break out of. Individuals may become trapped in a negative pattern of thinking and behavior, reinforcing their sense of helplessness and dependence on others. This can lead to a lack of agency and personal responsibility, making it difficult to take action and make changes in their lives.

As the victim mentality becomes more deeply ingrained, individuals may begin to see their circumstances as unchangeable and inevitable, further reinforcing their sense of powerlessness. They may become more isolated and disconnected from others, as their negative attitudes and beliefs can create barriers to forming healthy relationships.

Breaking out of the victim mentality requires a willingness to take personal responsibility for one's thoughts, feelings, and actions. It involves recognizing and challenging negative patterns of thinking and behavior, and making a conscious effort to focus on personal strengths and positive qualities. With time and effort, individuals can break free from the victim mentality and take control of their lives.

6. The Role of Empathy: Balancing Compassion with Personal Responsibility

Empathy is an essential component of healthy relationships and social interactions. It allows individuals to understand and relate to others' experiences and perspectives, fostering greater understanding and connection. However, empathy must be balanced with a sense of personal responsibility to avoid falling into a victim mentality. While it is important to acknowledge and validate one's emotions and experiences, it is equally important to take ownership of one's actions and choices. Without this balance, individuals may become trapped in a cycle of blaming external factors for their problems, rather than taking proactive steps to improve their situations. By cultivating both empathy and personal responsibility, individuals can build stronger relationships and a greater sense of agency in their lives.

Taking personal responsibility for one's actions and choices is a critical aspect of personal growth and development. It involves acknowledging one's role in creating their circumstances and actively working towards positive change. Individuals who take responsibility for their actions and choices are better equipped to deal with challenges and setbacks, as they have a sense of agency and control over their lives. By taking responsibility, individuals can also cultivate a sense of self-efficacy and confidence, which can lead to increased resilience and an overall sense of well-being. Ultimately, personal responsibility is an essential component of a healthy mindset and a fulfilling life.

Empathy is a valuable quality that allows individuals to connect with others and understand their experiences. However, it is essential to balance empathy with personal responsibility. It can be easy to fall into a victim mentality and blame external circumstances for one's problems, rather than taking ownership of one's actions and choices. While empathy can help individuals understand the challenges and hardships faced by others, it should not be used as an excuse to avoid taking responsibility for one's own life. In order to develop resilience and avoid victimhood, individuals must be willing to acknowledge their agency and take action to make positive changes in their lives.

Finding the right balance between empathy and personal responsibility is key to developing a growth mindset and achieving personal success. Empathy can help us understand and connect with others, leading to stronger relationships and a deeper understanding of the world around us. However, it's important not to let empathy overshadow our sense of personal responsibility. Taking ownership of our actions and choices allows us to develop resilience and learn from our mistakes, leading to personal growth and achievement. By cultivating both empathy and personal responsibility, we can create a positive mindset that allows us to thrive and reach our full potential.

Personal responsibility refers to the ability to take control of one's life and the outcomes of one's choices. It means acknowledging that our thoughts, emotions, and behaviors have consequences and that we are responsible for them. By accepting personal responsibility, individuals can gain a sense of agency and control over their lives, and develop resilience in the face of challenges and setbacks. It also means being accountable for our actions and making amends when necessary. Personal responsibility is a key component of personal growth and development, and it is essential for achieving success in any area of life.

Empathy is an important quality that allows individuals to understand and connect with the experiences of others. However, it is important to recognize that empathy should not be used as a way to avoid personal responsibility for one's own life. Taking ownership of one's thoughts, feelings, and actions is a crucial aspect of personal growth and development. It involves recognizing that we have agency in our own lives and that we have the power to make choices and take actions that can positively impact our circumstances. By taking personal responsibility, we can cultivate a sense of resilience and develop the skills necessary to navigate challenges and setbacks. While empathy is important for building strong relationships and understanding the experiences of others, it should be balanced with a sense of personal responsibility to achieve personal success and fulfillment.

Developing a sense of personal responsibility is an important step towards creating a fulfilling and successful life. It can be challenging to take ownership of one's actions and choices, especially when faced with difficult circumstances or setbacks. However, it is essential for building resilience and overcoming adversity. By acknowledging our own agency and ability to influence our lives, we can begin to make meaningful changes and move towards our goals. It is important to remember that personal responsibility is not about perfection, but rather a commitment to continuously learn, grow, and take action towards creating the life we want.

Empathy and compassion are critical qualities for building connections with others and supporting them during difficult times. However, it is important to recognize that empathy should not be used as a means of avoiding personal responsibility for one's own life. While it can be tempting to focus solely on the struggles and challenges faced by others, it is equally essential to take ownership of one's own thoughts, feelings, and actions. Developing a sense of personal responsibility involves recognizing the role that one's choices and behaviors play in shaping their life outcomes and taking proactive steps to create positive change. By balancing empathy with personal responsibility, individuals can build stronger relationships, cultivate resilience, and achieve greater success in their personal and professional lives.

Cultivating personal responsibility is an important aspect of personal growth and development. It involves taking ownership of one's choices and actions and recognizing the role that these factors play in shaping one's life. It means being accountable for one's decisions, and accepting the consequences that come with them. By acknowledging personal responsibility, individuals can take control of their lives and make positive changes. This can lead to increased self-esteem, resilience, and overall well-being. While it may be difficult to accept responsibility for one's actions, it is an essential step in personal growth and achieving success in life.

Empathy is a valuable tool for building connections with others and promoting understanding. However, it is crucial to maintain a balance between empathy and personal responsibility to avoid falling into a victim mentality. While it is important to be compassionate towards others, it is equally important to take control of one's own life and avoid blaming external factors or circumstances for one's problems. By cultivating a sense of personal responsibility, individuals can develop resilience and the ability to bounce back from adversity. They can also take proactive steps towards achieving their goals and living a fulfilling life. Ultimately, a healthy balance between empathy and personal responsibility can lead to greater happiness, success, and well-being.

Personal responsibility is a critical component of personal growth and success. By accepting responsibility for their choices and actions, individuals can take control of their lives and create positive change. This involves being proactive in identifying and pursuing goals, as well as being accountable for the consequences of one's decisions. Cultivating personal responsibility also requires a willingness to learn from mistakes and failures, and to use these experiences as opportunities for growth and self-improvement. Overall, taking ownership of one's life is a powerful tool for achieving personal fulfillment and reaching one's full potential.

Empathy and personal responsibility are two essential components for fostering positive relationships and achieving personal growth. Empathy helps individuals understand and connect with others, while personal responsibility involves taking ownership of one's actions and choices. When these two concepts are balanced, individuals can develop resilience and overcome challenges. Empathy allows individuals to recognize the experiences and perspectives of others, while personal responsibility empowers individuals to take control of their own lives and make positive changes. By balancing these two concepts, individuals can become more self-aware and compassionate towards others, while also taking ownership of their own well-being and success.

Taking personal responsibility for one's own life is a crucial component of developing resilience and achieving personal growth. It involves recognizing that one's choices and actions have an impact on one's life, rather than blaming external factors or circumstances for one's problems. By accepting personal responsibility, individuals can gain a sense of control over their lives and develop the skills and mindset necessary to overcome challenges and achieve success. It can be a difficult process, as it requires individuals to confront their own shortcomings and take ownership of their mistakes, but the benefits of personal responsibility are profound and long-lasting.

Empathy is a valuable trait that allows individuals to understand and connect with others, but it should not be used as a crutch to avoid personal responsibility. While it is important to recognize and validate the experiences and feelings of others, it is equally important to take ownership of one's own life. This involves acknowledging the impact of one's choices and actions, rather than blaming external factors or circumstances for one's problems. By taking responsibility for one's own life, individuals can develop a sense of agency and control, which is crucial for achieving personal growth and success. Balancing empathy with personal responsibility can help individuals develop resilience and overcome challenges, while also building strong, supportive relationships with others.

Empathy and personal responsibility are two essential elements that must be balanced in order to cultivate a sense of agency and achieve personal growth and success. Empathy allows us to understand and connect with others, to be more compassionate, and to develop meaningful relationships. However, it is important to avoid using empathy as an excuse for our own failures or shortcomings. Personal responsibility, on the other hand, involves taking ownership of our thoughts, feelings, and actions, and recognizing that we have the power to shape our lives through our choices. By taking responsibility for our lives, we can develop a sense of agency and control, and we can focus on making positive changes that will lead to personal growth and success. Ultimately, balancing empathy with personal responsibility allows us to develop a more holistic and fulfilling approach to life.

Personal responsibility is about taking ownership of one's own life and recognizing that one's choices and actions have a significant impact on their outcomes. It involves acknowledging one's agency and control over their life, rather than blaming external factors or circumstances for their problems. This means being accountable for one's own decisions and taking proactive steps towards achieving their goals. By cultivating personal responsibility, individuals can develop a greater sense of empowerment and resilience, and are better equipped to overcome obstacles and achieve personal growth and success.

Empathy is a crucial aspect of building strong relationships and fostering understanding between individuals. However, it is important to recognize that empathy should not be used as a way of avoiding personal responsibility. Empathy involves understanding and recognizing the experiences of others, but personal responsibility involves taking ownership of one's own choices and actions. By avoiding personal responsibility and relying solely on empathy, individuals may fall into a victim mentality and feel powerless to make positive changes in their own lives. Balancing empathy with personal responsibility is crucial for developing a growth mindset and achieving personal success.

Developing a sense of personal responsibility is a crucial step towards achieving personal growth and success. It requires individuals to take ownership of their own lives and recognize the role that their choices and actions play in shaping their experiences. Rather than blaming external factors or circumstances, individuals who cultivate personal responsibility are able to take control of their lives and make positive changes. This involves being honest with oneself, acknowledging mistakes and failures, and learning from them. By taking personal responsibility, individuals can develop a growth mindset, and overcome adversity to achieve their goals.

Empathy and personal responsibility are two important concepts that are often seen as opposing forces. Empathy involves understanding and connecting with others, while personal responsibility involves taking ownership of one's own choices and actions. Balancing these two concepts can be challenging, but it is essential for achieving personal growth and success. Empathy can help individuals develop a greater understanding of the experiences of others, but it should not be used as an excuse to avoid personal responsibility. Similarly, personal responsibility requires individuals to take ownership of their own lives and recognize the role that their choices and actions play in shaping their experiences. By balancing empathy with personal responsibility, individuals can develop a sense of agency and control over their own lives, and achieve greater resilience and success.

Personal responsibility is a fundamental aspect of personal growth and development. It requires individuals to take ownership of their own lives and recognize that their choices and actions play a significant role in shaping their experiences. When individuals take responsibility for their lives, they are empowered to make positive changes and pursue their goals with confidence. This can involve setting goals, making plans, and taking action to achieve those goals. By taking responsibility for their lives, individuals can develop a sense of agency and control that enables them to overcome challenges and obstacles, and ultimately achieve personal success.

7. The Attention Economy: How Victim Chic is a Product of Modern Culture

The Attention Economy is a term used to describe a marketplace in which attention is a valuable and limited resource. In this economy, companies compete to capture and hold the attention of consumers, often through various forms of advertising and marketing. This concept has become increasingly relevant with the rise of digital media and the internet, which have created new ways for businesses to vie for the attention of potential customers. As attention has become more fragmented and easily distracted, companies have had to adapt and find new ways to capture and retain their audiences. This has led to the development of innovative advertising and marketing techniques, as well as the rise of social media influencers and content creators who are able to command large audiences and capture their attention.

In today's digital age, attention is a scarce commodity. With so much information and content available at our fingertips, companies and individuals must constantly fight for the attention of their target audience. This has given rise to what is known as the Attention Economy, a market in which attention is a valuable and finite resource. In this economy, success depends on the ability to capture and hold people's attention amidst the noise of the digital world. To do this, companies must create engaging content and experiences that resonate with their audience, while individuals must carefully manage their own attention to avoid distraction and maintain focus on their goals.

Victim Chic is a term used to describe the phenomenon of individuals using their perceived victimhood as a means of gaining attention and sympathy from others. This can manifest in a variety of ways, from social media posts highlighting personal struggles to publicly airing grievances and seeking validation for one's experiences. While genuine victimization should be acknowledged and addressed, the pursuit of attention and validation through victimhood can be harmful, both to the individual and to society as a whole. It can reinforce a victim mentality and undermine personal agency, leading individuals to feel powerless and helpless in the face of adversity. Additionally, it can perpetuate a culture of victimhood, in which individuals compete for attention and validation through their experiences of victimization.

Social media has undoubtedly played a role in the rise of Victim Chic by providing a platform for individuals to share their stories and gain attention from others. Social media platforms such as Facebook, Twitter, and Instagram allow individuals to share their personal experiences and connect with others who may have had similar experiences. However, this has also created a culture in which victimhood is seen as a means of gaining attention and social status. This can be seen in the way that some individuals use social media to share their stories of victimization in a way that seems to glamorize their struggles and garner sympathy from others. While social media has the potential to be a powerful tool for connection and empowerment, it can also perpetuate a culture of victimhood and attention-seeking.

In the attention economy, the scarce resource of attention creates a competition for who can capture the most attention. This has led to the emergence of "victim chic," where individuals seek attention by portraying themselves as victims of various societal issues. Social media has further perpetuated this culture of victimhood, creating a platform for individuals to share their stories and gain attention from their followers. This can lead to a reinforcement of a victim mentality, where individuals view themselves as powerless and helpless victims rather than taking personal responsibility for their lives. The attention economy thus promotes and rewards the undesirable state of victimhood, rather than encouraging individuals to take control of their lives and seek personal growth and empowerment.

In the Attention Economy, where attention is a scarce resource, victimhood has become a valuable commodity. By portraying oneself as a victim, individuals and companies can capture attention, gain sympathy, and even profit from the resulting publicity. Social media has only exacerbated this trend, providing a platform for anyone to share their victimhood stories and compete for attention. As a result, victimhood has become a desirable state, leading many to exaggerate or even fabricate their victimhood experiences. This not only perpetuates a culture of victimhood but also undermines the genuine experiences of those who have truly suffered from oppression or discrimination.

The rise of reality TV and celebrity culture has contributed to the growth of the Attention Economy by promoting the idea that attention is the ultimate goal. Reality TV shows and social media platforms often focus on individuals seeking attention and fame, regardless of the means by which they achieve it. This has created a cultural shift in which people are more willing to do whatever it takes to get attention, including portraying themselves as victims. As a result, victimhood has become a valuable commodity in the Attention Economy, leading to the glorification of victimhood and the normalization of victim chic.

In the Attention Economy, victimhood has become a powerful tool for gaining attention and sympathy, which has led to a culture in which victimhood is often rewarded. As a result, there is a race to the bottom for who can claim the title of the biggest victim, rather than a focus on personal responsibility and agency. This race to victimhood can be seen in various aspects of society, from social media to politics, where individuals and groups seek to gain attention and support by positioning themselves as victims. However, this culture of victimhood ultimately undermines individual agency and personal responsibility, as it encourages individuals to blame external factors rather than taking ownership of their own lives.

Victim Chic can be seen as a response to the pressures of the Attention Economy, as individuals seek attention and validation through victimhood. In a culture where attention is the ultimate currency, some may feel compelled to use victimhood as a means of standing out and gaining recognition. This can lead to a vicious cycle where individuals compete to be the most victimized, rather than working to overcome challenges and take control of their own lives. Ultimately, this can be damaging both for individuals and for society as a whole, as it reinforces a culture of helplessness and victimization.

In the Attention Economy, victimhood has become a valuable commodity. Unfortunately, this has led to a devaluation of personal responsibility, as individuals may use victimhood as an excuse for their own shortcomings rather than taking ownership of their choices and actions. This can have negative consequences for individuals and society as a whole, as it undermines the values of resilience, self-improvement, and accountability. In a society where victimhood is celebrated, individuals may be less likely to take action to improve their own circumstances and more likely to look to external sources for solutions to their problems. Ultimately, a balance must be struck between recognizing and addressing legitimate issues of victimization and promoting personal responsibility and agency.

The prevalence of victimhood in the Attention Economy can have negative consequences, as it can perpetuate a sense of powerlessness and discourage individuals from taking control of their own lives. By promoting victimhood as a desirable state, individuals may become more focused on gaining attention and sympathy rather than on personal growth and development. Additionally, the devaluation of personal responsibility can lead to a lack of accountability, as individuals may use victimhood as an excuse for their own actions or inaction. Ultimately, it is important to recognize the potential dangers of the Attention Economy and its culture of victimhood, and to strive for a more balanced and responsible approach to gaining attention and validation.

In the Attention Economy, victimhood is often used as a means of gaining attention and sympathy, which can distract from the importance of personal responsibility and internal growth. This focus on external factors can be harmful, as it can prevent individuals from recognizing their own agency and taking proactive steps towards positive change. Additionally, the constant need for attention and validation can lead to a lack of focus on personal development and meaningful relationships. Overall, the culture of victimhood in the Attention Economy highlights the need for a shift towards personal responsibility and internal growth.

The Attention Economy has had a significant impact on the way people seek and receive attention. It has created a culture of entitlement, where individuals feel they are entitled to attention and sympathy based on their victimhood status. The desire for attention has led to a proliferation of victimhood narratives, and people often compete to be the biggest victim. This mentality can be harmful, as it can promote a sense of helplessness and entitlement, and discourage personal responsibility. In order to foster a healthier society, it is important to promote a culture of personal responsibility and accountability, and to encourage individuals to take control of their own lives.

The emphasis on victimhood in the Attention Economy can also lead to a lack of empathy and understanding for those who are truly suffering. When victimhood becomes a commodity to gain attention and sympathy, it can diminish the severity and importance of real experiences of trauma and injustice. Moreover, the constant portrayal of victimhood can desensitize people to the suffering of others, as well as create a "victim-blaming" mentality, where people assume that those who have experienced hardship are responsible for their own misfortune. Therefore, it is important to maintain a critical and discerning attitude towards victimhood in the Attention Economy, and to prioritize compassion and empathy for those who are truly struggling.

In the Attention Economy, outrage has become a valuable currency, as it generates engagement and attention. As a result, many individuals and groups have adopted a strategy of constant outrage, seeking to be the most offended and to garner the most attention. This has created a culture in which people are quick to take offense and to engage in public shaming, often without considering the nuances of the situation. The constant focus on outrage can also lead to a lack of empathy and understanding, as people become more focused on their own sense of victimhood than on the experiences of others. Overall, the culture of outrage in the Attention Economy can be damaging to individuals and to society as a whole.

Victim Chic, the practice of using victimhood as a means of gaining attention, can also be seen as a form of virtue signaling. By portraying themselves as victims, individuals can signal their moral superiority to others, positioning themselves as advocates for social justice and righteousness. However, this can also lead to a distortion of what true victimhood is and trivialize the experiences of those who are truly suffering. The practice of victim chic can also lead to a culture of one-upmanship, in which individuals compete to be seen as the most virtuous and moral, rather than focusing on meaningful action and positive change.

In the Attention Economy, victimhood can be weaponized as a means of gaining power and influence. This can lead to a toxic culture in which individuals use their victimhood status to attack and discredit others, rather than seeking understanding and empathy. The competitive nature of the Attention Economy can exacerbate this behavior, as individuals and groups vie for attention and validation. This can create a cycle of outrage and victimhood, in which each side seeks to outdo the other in their claims of victimhood and oppression. Ultimately, this can lead to a breakdown in communication and a lack of constructive dialogue, as individuals become more focused on gaining attention and sympathy than on finding solutions to the issues at hand.

In the Attention Economy, victimhood has become a form of currency, but it can also have negative consequences. The culture of victimhood in this economy can lead to a lack of personal agency and empowerment, as individuals see themselves as passive victims of circumstance. This mindset can be harmful, as it can prevent individuals from taking action to improve their own lives and achieve their goals. Instead of focusing on external factors, individuals should recognize the impact of their choices and actions on their own lives, and take ownership of their own success and well-being. This sense of personal responsibility is essential for cultivating a sense of agency and achieving personal growth and success.

The Attention Economy has created a world in which individuals must constantly compete for attention, leading to a culture of self-promotion and narcissism. Social media platforms have exacerbated this trend, with individuals curating their online personas to project a perfect image of themselves. The need for constant validation and attention can lead to a distorted sense of self-worth, as individuals tie their value to the number of likes, followers, and views they receive. This can result in a lack of authenticity and a focus on surface-level appearances rather than true personal growth and fulfillment. In the Attention Economy, being visible is often seen as more important than being genuine.

8. The Intersection of Identity: How Race, Gender, and Class Shape Victim Chic

Race, gender, and class are important factors that shape how victimhood is perceived and experienced in society. For example, individuals from marginalized communities may experience greater levels of victimization due to systemic inequalities and discrimination. Their experiences may be invalidated or dismissed due to their social status, leading to a sense of helplessness and lack of agency. On the other hand, individuals from privileged backgrounds may use victimhood as a means of gaining attention and sympathy, perpetuating the culture of victimhood in the Attention Economy. Understanding the intersectionality of these factors is essential for addressing the complex issues surrounding victimhood and the Attention Economy.

The intersection of identity can play a significant role in shaping how victimhood is perceived and experienced. Factors such as race, gender, class, sexuality, and ability can impact an individual's experiences of oppression and marginalization, and therefore their understanding of victimhood. For example, a Black woman may experience victimization differently than a white woman, due to the intersectionality of race and gender. Similarly, an individual with a disability may experience victimization differently than someone without a disability. These intersections can result in complex and nuanced understandings of victimhood that are shaped by both individual and societal factors. Understanding these intersections is important for creating more inclusive and equitable understandings of victimhood.

Historically marginalized groups, such as people of color, LGBTQ+ individuals, and those from low-income backgrounds, may be more likely to identify as victims due to systemic discrimination and oppression. These groups may have experienced exclusion and disadvantage in various aspects of life, including education, employment, and healthcare. As a result, they may have a heightened awareness of the ways in which their identities shape their experiences and the challenges they face. However, it is important to recognize that victimhood is not a monolithic experience and that individuals within these groups may have varying experiences and perspectives. Additionally, the Attention Economy may further complicate the relationship between identity and victimhood, as individuals may feel pressure to perform their victimhood in order to gain attention and validation.

The impact of identity on victimhood is complex and multifaceted, and can vary depending on a range of individual and societal factors. In some cases, individuals who belong to historically marginalized groups may be more likely to identify as victims due to systemic discrimination and oppression. However, the relationship between identity and victimhood is not always straightforward, and the impact of identity can vary depending on the cultural context and the specific experiences of individuals. For example, an individual's socio-economic status, religion, and sexual orientation may also shape their experience of victimhood, and may interact with their gender or race to create a unique set of challenges and opportunities. Ultimately, understanding the intersection of identity and victimhood requires a nuanced and inclusive approach that acknowledges the diversity of experiences within and across different groups.

The intersection of identity and victimhood can result in unique challenges for those seeking support and healing, as the impact of trauma can be shaped by cultural, historical, and social factors. Individuals may face additional barriers to accessing care and support due to systemic discrimination and marginalization. It is important for service providers to be aware of these intersections and to offer culturally sensitive approaches to treatment and therapy. This may include acknowledging the impact of societal factors such as racism and sexism, and working to create a safe and supportive environment for individuals to heal and recover. By recognizing and addressing the intersection of identity and victimhood, we can work towards creating a more inclusive and equitable society for all.

Intersectionality refers to the ways in which various forms of identity intersect to create unique experiences of oppression and privilege. When it comes to victimhood, the intersection of multiple forms of oppression can result in a greater impact on an individual's well-being and sense of agency. For example, an individual who experiences racism and sexism may be more vulnerable to gender-based violence, as well as racial discrimination in seeking support and justice. The impact of intersectionality on victimhood can be further exacerbated by factors such as class, ability, and sexuality, creating complex and multi-faceted experiences of harm. Recognizing and addressing the intersection of identity in victimhood is essential for creating more inclusive and effective systems of support and advocacy.

The intersection of identity and victimhood can also shape how individuals respond to experiences of victimization. For some, victimhood can be a means of resistance and empowerment, as they use their experiences to challenge oppressive systems and demand change. However, for others, the label of victim can be stigmatizing and disempowering, leading them to reject it altogether. The ways in which individuals navigate their experiences of victimization can be influenced by a range of factors, including cultural norms, personal beliefs, and access to resources and support. Thus, understanding the complex intersections of identity and victimhood is crucial for creating effective and equitable responses to victimization.

The intersection of identity and victimhood can lead to disparities in access to justice and resources, as marginalized groups may face additional barriers and obstacles in seeking support and redress for harm. For example, individuals from historically oppressed groups may be less likely to report victimization due to fear of discrimination or distrust of law enforcement. Additionally, systemic biases and prejudices within the justice system can result in unequal treatment and outcomes for different groups. Addressing these disparities and ensuring equal access to justice and resources for all individuals is crucial in creating a more just and equitable society.

The impact of identity on victimhood is not fixed, but is rather a dynamic and ever-changing process. As societal attitudes and cultural norms shift over time, so too can the way in which victimhood is experienced and understood. For example, what may have been perceived as a non-issue or even acceptable behavior in the past may now be viewed as a serious form of victimization. This can result in changes in laws, policies, and social norms to better protect and support those who have been victimized. At the same time, changes in social attitudes can also lead to new forms of victimization, highlighting the ongoing need for awareness, education, and advocacy.

Cultural attitudes towards identity and victimhood can have a profound impact on how individuals view themselves and others who have experienced harm. In some cultures, victimhood may be seen as a sign of weakness or vulnerability, leading to stigmatization and shame for those who come forward about their experiences. In other cultures, victimhood may be seen as a badge of honor, with individuals proudly asserting their status as survivors. These attitudes can shape how individuals perceive their own victimization and may impact their willingness to seek support and resources. It is important for cultural attitudes to shift towards a more empathetic and supportive view of victims, one that recognizes the complex intersection of identity and victimhood and prioritizes the needs and experiences of survivors.

The intersection of identity and victimhood can illuminate the complex relationships between power, privilege, and oppression. By recognizing the ways in which different forms of identity intersect and influence experiences of victimization, individuals and communities can work towards more intersectional approaches to social justice and activism. This includes acknowledging the ways in which privilege and power can impact one's experiences of victimization, as well as the ways in which marginalized groups may be further oppressed due to the intersection of multiple identities. An intersectional approach to social justice and activism seeks to address the root causes of systemic oppression and promote equity and justice for all individuals, regardless of their identities.

The impact of identity on victimhood can be shaped by internalized biases and stereotypes, as individuals may internalize societal messages about their identity and victimhood. For example, individuals from historically marginalized groups may internalize beliefs about their own inferiority, leading them to view victimhood as a natural state of being. On the other hand, individuals from privileged groups may internalize beliefs about their own superiority, leading them to deny or minimize the experiences of others. Recognizing and confronting these internalized biases and stereotypes is a crucial step in developing a more nuanced and compassionate understanding of victimhood. It also highlights the importance of ongoing self-awareness and personal growth in creating a more just and equitable society.

The intersection of identity and victimhood can result in individuals feeling disconnected from their communities and struggling to find a sense of belonging. Those who experience victimization that is not recognized or acknowledged within their cultural context may feel particularly isolated. This can lead to feelings of shame and self-blame, as well as a reluctance to seek support or speak out about their experiences. It is important for communities to create spaces that are inclusive and affirming of all individuals, and to actively work to combat stigma and discrimination. Only then can we begin to address the complex and multifaceted impact of identity on victimhood.

The intersection of identity and victimhood can create complex and nuanced experiences of trauma and healing. In seeking to heal from trauma, individuals may face unique challenges related to their intersecting identities, including barriers to accessing culturally sensitive treatment and the potential for compounded stigma and discrimination. For example, a person who experiences both racism and homophobia may struggle to find a therapist who understands their experiences and can provide effective support. It is crucial for mental health professionals to recognize and address the ways in which identity intersects with victimhood in order to provide inclusive and effective care.

The impact of identity on victimhood can also be further complicated by other factors such as age, religion, and sexual orientation, resulting in a complex web of intersecting identities and experiences. For example, an older person who identifies as a member of a racial or ethnic minority may have experienced discrimination and victimization throughout their life, but may also face unique challenges related to aging, such as ageism and social isolation. Similarly, a queer person who also identifies as a person of color may experience discrimination and victimization related to both their sexual orientation and their race. The complexity of these intersections highlights the need for a more nuanced understanding of victimhood that takes into account the many ways in which identity can shape our experiences.

The intersection of identity and victimhood can lead to internal conflicts and contradictions, as individuals grapple with the complexity of their experiences and the societal expectations and norms placed upon them. For example, a person who identifies as both a woman and a member of a racial minority group may struggle to determine whether their experiences of discrimination are due to their gender or their race. Similarly, a person who identifies as a member of the LGBTQ+ community may feel pressure to downplay experiences of victimization in order to fit into mainstream society's expectations of gender and sexuality. These conflicts can lead to feelings of confusion, shame, and isolation, further complicating the healing process.

The intersection of identity and victimhood can be further influenced by various factors, including language, geography, and immigration status, which can shape individuals' experiences of victimization and their access to resources and support. For instance, language barriers can make it challenging for individuals to seek help and communicate their needs, while geographic location can affect the availability of services and support networks. Additionally, immigration status can increase vulnerability to certain forms of victimization, such as exploitation and abuse, while also limiting access to legal protections and resources. To address these complexities, intersectional approaches to policy and advocacy are needed to ensure that marginalized communities are adequately supported and represented.

The impact of identity on victimhood can be further shaped by various factors, such as mental health, disability, and addiction. Individuals who are already marginalized due to their identity may be further stigmatized and face additional barriers in accessing support and resources when dealing with mental health challenges, disabilities, or addiction. This can result in a complex and layered experience of victimhood, with intersecting identities and experiences compounding each other. It highlights the need for a holistic and intersectional approach to addressing victimization and promoting healing, taking into account the multiple facets of an individual's identity and experiences.

The intersection of identity and victimhood can have a significant impact on whose stories and experiences are heard and valued in society. Marginalized groups may face greater barriers to having their voices heard and their experiences recognized, while dominant groups may have their victimhood more readily acknowledged and amplified. This highlights the importance of inclusive and diverse representation in media and public discourse, as well as the need for intersectional approaches to understanding and addressing issues of victimization. By acknowledging and valuing the experiences of individuals across the intersections of identity, we can work towards a more equitable and just society for all.

9. The Paradox of Privilege: Recognizing and Addressing Our Own Biases

Privilege refers to a set of unearned advantages and benefits conferred upon individuals by society based on their social identity, such as race, gender, class, sexual orientation, and ability status. These advantages are often invisible to those who hold them, as they are perceived as the norm and are taken for granted. Privilege can manifest in many ways, such as easier access to opportunities, greater representation in media and politics, and less discrimination and prejudice. However, the existence of privilege can also lead to the marginalization and oppression of those who do not hold these advantages, perpetuating systemic inequalities and injustice. Recognizing privilege and working to dismantle systems of oppression is crucial for creating a more equitable and just society.

Privilege can manifest in different forms depending on an individual's social identity. Economic privilege, for example, refers to the advantages and benefits that come with wealth and financial stability. Racial privilege refers to the unearned advantages and benefits that come with being a member of a dominant racial group within a society. Gender privilege refers to the societal advantages and benefits that come with being perceived as male within a patriarchal society. Similarly, sexual orientation privilege refers to the societal advantages and benefits that come with being perceived as heterosexual within a heteronormative society. Each form of privilege can intersect with other forms of identity to create complex and nuanced experiences of power and oppression.

Privilege can be difficult to recognize and acknowledge, especially for those who possess it. This is because privilege often goes unnoticed by those who benefit from it, as it is considered the norm and taken for granted. It can be challenging to see how one's identity and social position have granted them unearned advantages and benefits, as it is not always immediately visible or tangible. However, recognizing and acknowledging privilege is crucial for creating a more equitable and just society, as it allows individuals to understand and challenge the systems and structures that perpetuate inequality.

Recognizing and acknowledging privilege is crucial in addressing and dismantling systemic inequalities. It requires individuals to reflect on their own experiences and the advantages they may have received based on their social identity. This process can be uncomfortable and even painful, as it may challenge deeply held beliefs and assumptions about oneself and society. However, it is necessary in order to understand and address the ways in which privilege operates in systems and institutions. By acknowledging and actively working to address privilege, individuals can become allies in the fight for equity and social justice.

Privilege can be perpetuated through unconscious biases and discriminatory practices that favor those who hold certain social identities over others. For example, hiring managers may unconsciously favor job candidates who share their race, gender, or socioeconomic background, resulting in a lack of diversity in the workplace. Similarly, laws and policies that favor certain groups, such as tax breaks for the wealthy, can perpetuate economic privilege and widen the gap between the rich and poor. It is important to be aware of these biases and practices in order to challenge and change them, creating a more equitable society for all.

Privilege can indeed create a sense of entitlement and a lack of accountability for one's actions. When individuals possess certain privileges based on their social identity, they may be less likely to recognize the impact of their actions on those who do not share their privileges. This can lead to a lack of accountability and responsibility for the harm caused, as well as a reluctance to acknowledge the privileges that contributed to their actions. Moreover, privilege can also foster a sense of superiority and complacency, perpetuating the status quo and hindering progress towards social justice and equality. Recognizing and confronting one's own privilege is crucial in promoting a more equitable and just society.

Recognizing and addressing one's own privilege can be a difficult and uncomfortable process. It requires self-reflection, self-awareness, and a willingness to acknowledge the ways in which societal systems and structures have privileged certain groups over others. However, this process is necessary for personal growth and for creating a more just and equitable society. By acknowledging and addressing one's own privilege, individuals can begin to understand how their actions and behaviors may contribute to systemic inequality, and take steps to challenge and dismantle these systems. It is important to approach this process with humility and a willingness to listen to and learn from those who have experienced oppression and marginalization.

Privilege can lead to a lack of empathy and understanding towards those who do not possess the same advantages. When individuals are accustomed to certain privileges and benefits, they may struggle to comprehend the experiences of those who face systemic barriers and discrimination. This can result in a lack of empathy and a dismissive attitude towards the struggles of marginalized communities. It is important to acknowledge and address these attitudes in order to foster greater understanding and compassion towards those who experience different forms of oppression and disadvantage. By actively working to broaden our perspectives and educate ourselves on the experiences of others, we can build a more inclusive and equitable society.

The intersection of multiple forms of privilege can result in a complex web of advantages and disadvantages faced by individuals. For example, a wealthy, white, cisgender, heterosexual man may experience economic, racial, gender, and sexual orientation privilege, while also facing certain challenges due to his disability or mental health status. Similarly, a wealthy, white, cisgender, heterosexual woman may experience economic and racial privilege, while facing challenges related to gender and sexual orientation. Recognizing the ways in which multiple forms of privilege intersect is crucial for understanding the ways in which power and oppression operate in society, and for working towards greater equity and social justice.

Addressing privilege requires active listening, humility, and a willingness to learn from marginalized communities. It involves examining and challenging one's own biases and assumptions, as well as actively working towards creating a more equitable and just society. This can include supporting policies and initiatives that prioritize marginalized communities, using one's own privilege to uplift marginalized voices, and advocating for systemic change. It is important to recognize that addressing privilege is an ongoing process that requires consistent reflection and action. It can be uncomfortable and challenging, but it is necessary for promoting equity and social justice.

Privilege can be used as a tool for advocacy and allyship by those who possess it. By acknowledging and using their advantages, individuals can work towards amplifying the voices and experiences of marginalized communities. This can include advocating for policy changes, supporting and funding grassroots organizations, and using their platforms and networks to elevate underrepresented voices. It is important, however, for individuals to center the perspectives and needs of the communities they are supporting, rather than centering themselves. Effective allyship requires active listening, learning, and amplification of marginalized voices, as well as a commitment to ongoing self-reflection and accountability.

Privilege can indeed lead to a distorted view of reality, as individuals who possess it may not fully understand or acknowledge the systemic barriers and discrimination faced by marginalized communities. This lack of awareness can result in a narrow perspective that fails to recognize the experiences and perspectives of others. It is important for individuals with privilege to actively seek out diverse perspectives and experiences, listen to marginalized voices, and engage in ongoing education and advocacy efforts to address and dismantle systemic inequalities. Only by recognizing and addressing privilege can we work towards a more just and equitable society.

Privilege can create a sense of complacency and a lack of urgency to address systemic issues, as those who benefit from existing power structures may not see the need for change. This can perpetuate inequality and perpetuate the marginalization of already vulnerable communities. It is important for individuals with privilege to actively engage in efforts to promote equity and justice, and to listen to the perspectives and experiences of those who are directly impacted by systemic oppression. Only by acknowledging and addressing privilege can we work towards a more just and equitable society for all.

Recognizing privilege is an important step towards promoting equity and social justice. It is important to note that acknowledging one's privilege is not an indictment of one's character or personal achievements, but rather an acknowledgment of the systemic advantages that are conferred by society based on one's social identity. It is crucial to approach the topic of privilege with humility, active listening, and a willingness to learn from marginalized communities. By recognizing and addressing privilege, individuals can work towards creating a more just and equitable society for all.

Privilege can certainly bring up feelings of guilt and shame, especially when one becomes aware of the advantages they have had in life that others do not have. However, it's important to remember that these feelings are a natural part of the process of recognizing and addressing privilege, and that it's okay to feel uncomfortable or even embarrassed about it. The key is to use those feelings as a motivator for positive action, rather than becoming mired in them. It's also important to remember that the goal is not to deny or minimize one's own advantages, but rather to use them to work towards a more just and equitable society for all. This means acknowledging and addressing privilege, and working in partnership with marginalized communities to create lasting change.

Addressing privilege requires a commitment to ongoing self-reflection and education. It involves actively seeking out diverse perspectives and experiences, engaging in critical self-examination, and being open to feedback and criticism. It also requires taking responsibility for one's actions and using one's privilege to advocate for marginalized communities. This process can be challenging and uncomfortable, but it is essential for creating a more equitable and just society. It requires a willingness to listen, learn, and evolve, and a recognition that the work of dismantling systemic inequality is ongoing and requires sustained effort.

Privilege is a complex and multifaceted concept that can present challenges to individuals seeking to address systemic inequalities. However, recognizing and addressing one's privilege can also be an opportunity for personal growth and social change. By acknowledging the advantages conferred by society based on one's social identity, individuals can become more aware of their own biases and work towards dismantling oppressive systems. Additionally, using one's privilege as a tool for advocacy and allyship can amplify marginalized voices and bring about meaningful change. While addressing privilege can be uncomfortable and challenging, it is necessary for creating a more just and equitable society for all.

Recognizing and addressing privilege is a complex and ongoing process that requires a long-term commitment to systemic change. It is not enough to engage in individual acts of charity or tokenism, as this can often perpetuate unequal power dynamics. Instead, individuals must be willing to actively listen, learn, and engage in meaningful actions that challenge systemic inequalities. This may include supporting marginalized communities, advocating for policy change, and holding institutions accountable for their actions. It also requires an understanding that addressing privilege is not a one-time event, but rather a continuous process of reflection and action. Ultimately, dismantling systemic inequalities requires a collective effort towards creating a more just and equitable society for all.

Privilege can perpetuate a cycle of victimhood, as individuals may attribute their successes solely to their own efforts, rather than acknowledging the advantages and opportunities afforded to them by society. This can lead to a sense of superiority and a lack of empathy towards those who have not had the same advantages, perpetuating the idea of victimhood as a personal failing rather than a systemic issue. It is important to recognize the role that privilege plays in shaping individual outcomes, and to work towards creating a more equitable and just society for all. By acknowledging privilege and actively working to dismantle systemic inequalities, we can break the cycle of victimhood and promote a more inclusive and compassionate society.

Addressing privilege is not only an individual responsibility, but also a collective one. It requires a commitment to dismantling systemic barriers that perpetuate inequality and promoting policies and practices that promote justice and equity for all individuals. This involves engaging in critical dialogue and activism, challenging discriminatory practices and policies, and promoting inclusive and diverse representation in all spheres of society. By working together to address privilege and promote social justice, we can create a more just and equitable society for all.

10. The Media's Role in Victim Chic: How News and Entertainment Feed the Narrative

News media has been criticized for prioritizing stories of victimization that are sensational and emotionally charged, often leading to a skewed representation of reality. This is because these stories are more likely to capture the attention of audiences and generate higher ratings and revenue for media outlets. However, the overemphasis on victimhood can also lead to a limited and narrow understanding of complex social issues and reinforce negative stereotypes and biases. It is important for news media to prioritize accurate and nuanced reporting that takes into account the diverse experiences and perspectives of marginalized communities, and to avoid perpetuating harmful narratives that can further marginalize and harm vulnerable populations.

The media's emphasis on victimhood can inadvertently undermine personal responsibility and contribute to a mentality of learned helplessness. When news outlets predominantly highlight stories of individuals facing adversities and injustices, there is a risk of downplaying the agency and resilience of individuals in overcoming challenges. This constant exposure to victimization narratives can create a belief that one's circumstances are solely determined by external factors, leading to a diminished sense of personal responsibility. While it is essential to acknowledge and address systemic issues, it is equally important to promote a balanced narrative that recognizes the role of personal agency and the capacity for individuals to take control of their own lives. By fostering a culture of empowerment and self-determination, we can encourage individuals to embrace personal responsibility and work towards positive change.

News and entertainment media have the power to shape public perception and influence societal attitudes. Unfortunately, in their portrayal of victims and perpetrators, media can perpetuate stereotypes and biases. Certain groups may be disproportionately depicted as victims, reinforcing negative stereotypes and further marginalizing these communities. Similarly, certain individuals or communities may be unfairly portrayed as perpetrators, reinforcing existing biases and prejudices.

This distorted representation not only perpetuates harmful stereotypes but also hinders efforts to foster understanding, empathy, and social cohesion. It is crucial for media organizations to prioritize diverse and accurate representations, challenging stereotypes, and promoting a more nuanced understanding of the complexities surrounding victimhood and perpetration. By doing so, media can play a pivotal role in fostering a more inclusive and equitable society.

The media plays a significant role in shaping public discourse and influencing the collective understanding of victimhood. However, at times, the media's framing of victimhood can inadvertently fuel public outrage and create a demand for immediate retribution, rather than a more nuanced approach that focuses on prevention and healing. Sensationalized and emotionally charged stories may prioritize the need for punishment and justice, often overshadowing the importance of addressing underlying causes and working towards long-term solutions. This emphasis on retribution can perpetuate a cycle of anger and division, hindering efforts to foster empathy, understanding, and restorative justice. It is crucial for the media to provide balanced and comprehensive coverage that not only highlights the experiences of victims but also promotes thoughtful reflection and constructive dialogue aimed at preventing future harm and promoting healing for all parties involved.

The media's emphasis on victimhood can have unintended consequences, contributing to the creation of a culture of fear and mistrust. When stories of victimhood are disproportionately highlighted, it can create a skewed perception of reality, leading individuals to perceive the world as a constant threat. This culture of fear can further isolate and divide communities, fostering a lack of empathy and understanding towards others. Instead of promoting dialogue and unity, it can perpetuate stereotypes, deepen divisions, and hinder meaningful connections. It is crucial for the media to strike a balance by providing a broader range of narratives that not only focus on victimhood but also highlight stories of resilience, empathy, and collective efforts to overcome challenges. By doing so, the media can help foster a culture of compassion, understanding, and unity, enabling individuals to empathize with the experiences of others and work towards a more inclusive and harmonious society.

News media has a tendency to sensationalize the experiences of victims, placing a heavy emphasis on the traumatic aspects rather than highlighting the resilience and healing that can follow. While it is important to shed light on the challenges and injustices faced by individuals, an excessive focus on sensationalizing victimhood can overshadow the stories of strength, growth, and recovery. By prioritizing shocking and emotionally charged narratives, the media can inadvertently perpetuate a one-dimensional portrayal of victims, failing to capture the complexity and diversity of their experiences. This emphasis on trauma alone can limit the public's understanding of the multifaceted nature of victimhood and overlook the transformative power of healing and resilience. It is crucial for the media to strike a balance by also sharing stories of hope, empowerment, and the journey towards healing. By doing so, they can contribute to a more comprehensive and nuanced understanding of victimhood, while offering inspiration and encouragement to those who have faced adversity.

The media's coverage of high-profile cases of victimization can have a profound impact on society. While it is essential for the media to report on such incidents to inform the public, there is a risk of inadvertently promoting copycat crimes and fostering an atmosphere of fear. Extensive coverage and sensationalized narratives can glamorize acts of victimization, potentially inspiring individuals who seek attention or notoriety. Moreover, constant exposure to these stories can amplify public anxiety and contribute to a pervasive sense of insecurity. It is crucial for the media to strike a balance between providing accurate information and responsible reporting to prevent the unintended consequences of fearmongering and increased vulnerability.

Entertainment media has a powerful influence on shaping societal narratives and perceptions. In some cases, it can perpetuate a culture of victimhood through the portrayal of characters who constantly depend on others for rescue and validation. These characters often lack agency and personal responsibility, reinforcing the notion that individuals are helpless victims of circumstance. By romanticizing and glorifying this dynamic, entertainment media can inadvertently contribute to the normalization of victimhood as a desirable state. Such portrayals may undermine the importance of self-empowerment, resilience, and the pursuit of personal growth. It is essential for the media industry to recognize the impact of these narratives and strive for a more balanced representation that encourages viewers to embrace their own agency and actively participate in their own lives.

The media plays a crucial role in shaping public discourse and influencing the social agenda. However, its excessive focus on victimization can sometimes overshadow more pressing social issues and potential solutions. By sensationalizing individual cases of victimhood, the media may inadvertently divert attention away from systemic problems and structural inequalities that perpetuate such victimization. This narrow focus on isolated incidents can hinder meaningful discussions and actions to address the root causes of social issues. It is important for the media to not only highlight victimization but also provide comprehensive coverage that explores the underlying factors and possible remedies. By broadening the scope of coverage and highlighting the complexities of social issues, the media can contribute to a more informed and nuanced public dialogue, fostering a greater understanding of the broader context and promoting effective solutions.

The media has a tendency to simplify and frame victimhood as a black-and-white issue, often presenting victims as wholly innocent and perpetrators as entirely culpable. While this approach may make for compelling narratives, it fails to capture the nuances and complexities of victimization. In reality, victims and perpetrators often exist on a spectrum, and the circumstances surrounding their experiences can be multifaceted. By oversimplifying the narrative, the media perpetuates a limited understanding of victimization, which can hinder the public's ability to comprehend the underlying causes and dynamics at play. It is crucial for the media to take a more nuanced approach, exploring the various factors and power dynamics that contribute to victimization, in order to foster a deeper understanding and empathy towards those affected by it. This more nuanced portrayal can help challenge stereotypes, address systemic issues, and promote a more comprehensive understanding of victimhood in society.

The media's emphasis on individual stories of victimization, while important for highlighting personal experiences and humanizing the impact of crime and injustice, can inadvertently obscure the larger systemic issues at play. By focusing solely on individual cases, the media may overlook the underlying social, economic, and political factors that contribute to victimization on a broader scale. These systemic issues can include inequality, poverty, discrimination, and the shortcomings of institutions responsible for ensuring safety and justice. By not contextualizing individual stories within these broader systemic frameworks, the media runs the risk of perpetuating a limited understanding of victimization and hindering efforts to address its root causes. It is crucial for the media to strike a balance, telling individual stories while also investigating and highlighting the structural factors that contribute to victimization. This comprehensive approach can promote a more informed and nuanced understanding of the issues at hand, leading to meaningful discussions and actions towards systemic change.

The media's constant rehashing of the experiences of victims can exacerbate their trauma and perpetuate a narrative of helplessness and victimhood. While it is essential to bring attention to instances of victimization and raise awareness about the impact of trauma, the media's repetitive coverage and sensationalized portrayals can be counterproductive. Continuous exposure to distressing details and reliving the traumatic events can retraumatize victims, impede their healing process, and reinforce feelings of powerlessness. Moreover, focusing solely on the victim's trauma may overshadow their resilience, strength, and ability to overcome adversity. It is crucial for the media to strike a balance by providing support, resources, and positive narratives of survivors, allowing them to reclaim their agency and highlight their journey towards healing and empowerment. By doing so, the media can contribute to a more compassionate and holistic understanding of victimhood while respecting the well-being and dignity of those affected.

The media's emphasis on victimhood can contribute to a culture of blame and retribution, diverting attention from essential aspects such as prevention and healing. By sensationalizing stories of victimization, the media often amplifies feelings of anger, resentment, and a desire for punishment. This focus on assigning blame and seeking retribution can overshadow the urgent need for prevention strategies that address root causes and systemic issues. While it is crucial to hold perpetrators accountable for their actions, a comprehensive approach to addressing victimization should include efforts to understand the underlying factors, promote empathy, and prioritize prevention measures. By shifting the narrative towards prevention and healing, the media can play a vital role in fostering a more compassionate and constructive discourse that seeks to address the systemic issues contributing to victimization and create a safer and more supportive society for all.

The media's emphasis on victimhood can indeed contribute to a culture of political polarization and identity politics. By framing issues through the lens of victimhood, the media can inadvertently reinforce divisions within society based on political ideologies or identity groups. This can lead to a heightened sense of "us versus them" mentality, where individuals align themselves with specific victimized groups and use their victimhood status as a tool for political mobilization or advocacy. The media's portrayal of victimhood often focuses on the grievances and injustices experienced by certain groups, amplifying their sense of collective victimization. This can further entrench divisions and hinder meaningful dialogue and understanding between different groups. To foster a more inclusive and cohesive society, it is important for the media to also highlight stories of resilience, collaboration, and shared humanity, and to promote narratives that encourage empathy and bridge the gaps between diverse perspectives. By doing so, the media can play a vital role in mitigating the negative effects of a culture centered around political polarization and identity politics.

11. The Power of Language: How Our Words Can Reduce Victimhood and Promote Empowerment

The power of language cannot be underestimated when it comes to shaping our perceptions of victimhood. The words we use to describe and discuss victimhood have the ability to either reinforce a sense of helplessness and dependency or foster a mindset of resilience and empowerment. By consciously choosing our language, we have the potential to transform how we perceive and respond to experiences of victimhood. Words that emphasize strength, agency, and growth can inspire individuals to overcome adversity, while language that perpetuates a victim mentality may reinforce feelings of powerlessness. Recognizing the transformative impact of language allows us to challenge societal narratives and narratives we tell ourselves, creating a space for individuals to reclaim their power and embrace a narrative of empowerment and resilience.

Inclusive and empowering language plays a crucial role in promoting a shift from victimhood to resilience. By using language that acknowledges and respects individual experiences while emphasizing strength and agency, we can create a supportive and empowering environment for those who have faced adversity. Inclusive language ensures that individuals feel seen, heard, and validated, fostering a sense of belonging and empowerment. Moreover, by reframing narratives and focusing on resilience, we encourage individuals to tap into their inner strength, to view challenges as opportunities for growth, and to develop a mindset that transcends the limitations of victimhood. By consciously choosing our words, we can inspire and uplift, creating a culture that celebrates personal agency and fosters a collective commitment to resilience and empowerment.

Language plays a significant role in reframing experiences and fostering a sense of personal agency. The words we use to describe our experiences and challenges can shape our perception of ourselves and the world around us. By consciously choosing empowering and affirmative language, we can reframe our narratives and take ownership of our experiences. Instead of casting ourselves as passive victims, we can use language that highlights our resilience, strength, and capacity for growth. This shift in language empowers us to see ourselves as active participants in our lives, capable of making choices and effecting change. By acknowledging our personal agency through the power of language, we can cultivate a sense of control and empowerment, transforming our experiences from ones of victimhood to ones of strength and possibility.

Language has the remarkable power to empower individuals, allowing them to take control of their narratives and challenge the notion of victimhood. By consciously choosing and using language that affirms their agency and resilience, individuals can redefine their experiences and reshape their identities. When individuals embrace language that emphasizes their strengths, accomplishments, and ability to overcome obstacles, they shift their focus from a passive victim mentality to an active and empowered mindset. By reframing their narratives, individuals reclaim their stories and challenge the limitations that victimhood imposes. Language becomes a tool for self-empowerment, enabling individuals to embrace their personal power, assert their autonomy, and rewrite their narratives on their own terms. This transformative use of language liberates individuals from the constraints of victimhood and fosters a sense of personal growth, resilience, and empowerment.

Language has the remarkable capacity to foster empathy and understanding, serving as a powerful tool for shifting perspectives and dismantling the victim mentality. By using language that promotes compassion, empathy, and active listening, we can create spaces for genuine connection and dialogue. By encouraging individuals to share their experiences and challenges in a way that highlights their resilience and strength, language can help break down barriers and bridge divides. Rather than perpetuating a victim mentality, the intentional use of language can promote a deeper understanding of the complexities of human experiences. It encourages us to see beyond labels and stereotypes, cultivating empathy and fostering a culture of support and empowerment. Through thoughtful and inclusive language, we can create a more compassionate society that recognizes the diverse narratives of individuals and fosters a shared sense of understanding and unity.

The power of language extends beyond shaping perceptions and narratives; it also plays a crucial role in promoting mental and emotional well-being. Empowering language can have a transformative impact on individuals' self-perception and overall outlook on life. By using language that affirms and uplifts, we can cultivate a positive and resilient mindset. Words that inspire hope, encourage personal growth, and validate individual experiences can contribute to a sense of self-worth and confidence. Empowering language can help individuals reframe their thoughts, break free from negative cycles, and embrace their strengths and capabilities. It can foster a sense of agency, reminding individuals that they have the power to overcome challenges and create meaningful change in their lives. Moreover, empowering language can create a supportive and inclusive environment that promotes emotional well-being, fostering a sense of belonging and connection. By using language that recognizes and celebrates individuals' strengths, resilience, and capacity for growth, we can contribute to a culture of mental and emotional well-being, where individuals feel empowered to navigate life's challenges and pursue their aspirations with confidence and optimism.

Language holds immense power in shaping social norms and attitudes towards victimhood. The words we use and the narratives we construct have the ability to either reinforce or challenge prevailing beliefs and perceptions. Through language, we can shape the collective understanding of victimhood, moving beyond stereotypes and misconceptions. By choosing our words carefully, we can promote empathy, compassion, and a deeper understanding of the experiences of those who have been victimized. Language has the capacity to challenge victim-blaming narratives, shift the focus from judgment to support, and foster a culture of accountability and justice. Moreover, by using language that emphasizes resilience, empowerment, and the potential for healing and growth, we can inspire a shift in social attitudes, encouraging a more compassionate and proactive response to victimhood. Language acts as a catalyst for change, as it not only reflects but also shapes societal norms and beliefs. Through conscious and intentional use of language, we can contribute to a more inclusive, empathetic, and supportive society that recognizes the dignity, worth, and agency of all individuals, regardless of their experiences of victimhood.

Language holds tremendous power in shaping the culture we inhabit, and it is through language that we can create a culture that celebrates strength and resilience. The words we choose to use can either reinforce narratives of victimhood or promote narratives of strength and empowerment. By embracing language that acknowledges the challenges individuals face while emphasizing their ability to overcome adversity, we can foster a culture that celebrates resilience. Through uplifting and empowering language, we can inspire individuals to tap into their inner strength, cultivate a sense of agency, and view themselves as active agents in their own lives rather than passive victims of circumstance. This shift in language not only influences individuals' self-perception but also shapes societal attitudes and perceptions, creating a collective understanding that values and uplifts strength and resilience. By using language that celebrates triumphs, highlights personal growth, and encourages collective support, we can foster a culture that recognizes and honors the resilience of individuals, creating an environment that inspires and uplifts all members of our society.

Overcoming victimhood requires a conscious choice to use empowering words and narratives. Language plays a significant role in shaping our thoughts, beliefs, and actions. By consciously reframing our experiences and adopting empowering narratives, we can break free from the limitations of victimhood. Instead of focusing solely on our past traumas or hardships, we can choose to highlight our resilience, strength, and ability to rise above adversity. Through empowering language, we can shift our mindset from a passive victim to an active agent, reclaiming our power and taking ownership of our lives. By choosing words that reflect our growth, potential, and capacity for change, we create a positive narrative that propels us forward. This shift in language not only transforms our own perception of ourselves but also influences how others perceive and interact with us. By consciously choosing empowering words and narratives, we can transcend victimhood, inspire others, and create a path towards personal empowerment and fulfillment.

The media and public discourse have a crucial responsibility in using language that fosters empowerment rather than victimization. The words and narratives conveyed through these channels have a profound impact on shaping societal attitudes and perceptions. By employing language that focuses on resilience, strength, and agency, the media can inspire individuals to overcome challenges and pursue their goals. Instead of perpetuating a culture of victimhood, the media can choose to highlight stories of empowerment, showcasing individuals who have triumphed over adversity and thrived despite their circumstances. By using inclusive and empowering language, the media can create a space that encourages dialogue, empathy, and understanding, fostering a sense of unity and collective empowerment. Recognizing their influential role, the media and public discourse have the power to shape narratives that promote personal growth, resilience, and societal progress. It is essential for these platforms to prioritize language that uplifts, empowers, and encourages individuals to embrace their inherent capabilities and potential.

Language has the incredible power to break the cycle of victimhood and foster a mindset of growth and self-empowerment. By consciously choosing words that focus on strength, resilience, and possibility, individuals can reshape their narratives and transcend the limitations of victimhood. Empowering language encourages a shift from a passive mindset to an active one, where individuals take ownership of their experiences and choices. It promotes the belief that challenges can be overcome, and setbacks can be seen as opportunities for growth and learning. By embracing language that promotes personal agency and self-empowerment, individuals can cultivate a mindset that is focused on progress, self-development, and the pursuit of their goals. Through the power of language, the cycle of victimhood can be broken, enabling individuals to rewrite their stories with determination, resilience, and a belief in their own ability to create positive change in their lives.

Language serves as a powerful tool to challenge societal stereotypes and biases associated with victimhood. By intentionally using inclusive and empowering language, individuals can disrupt and dismantle harmful narratives that perpetuate stereotypes and reinforce victimization. Through conscious efforts to choose words that promote equality, respect, and understanding, we can challenge the assumptions and biases that exist within society. Language can be used to humanize and dignify individuals who have experienced victimization, shifting the narrative from one of pity or blame to one of empathy and support. By actively challenging and redefining the language used to discuss victimhood, we can foster a more compassionate and inclusive society that recognizes the agency, resilience, and strength of individuals, and encourages their full participation and empowerment.

Positive self-talk and affirming language have a profound impact on personal empowerment. The words we choose to speak to ourselves shape our beliefs, attitudes, and actions. By consciously using uplifting and encouraging language, we can cultivate a mindset of self-belief, resilience, and determination. Positive self-talk reinforces our strengths, affirms our capabilities, and reminds us of our inherent worth. It serves as a powerful internal resource, boosting our confidence, motivation, and overall well-being. By reframing negative thoughts and replacing self-limiting language with empowering affirmations, we can overcome self-doubt, embrace our potential, and navigate challenges with a sense of optimism and self-assurance. The impact of positive self-talk extends beyond our inner world, as it influences how we present ourselves to the world and interact with others. By harnessing the power of affirming language, we can unlock our true potential, overcome obstacles, and embark on a journey of personal empowerment and growth.

The use of language plays a crucial role in creating a sense of community and support for individuals seeking to move beyond victimhood. By employing inclusive and empathetic language, we can foster an environment of understanding, validation, and encouragement. Language has the power to convey empathy, to acknowledge the experiences and emotions of others, and to create a safe space for healing and growth. When we choose our words with care, we can communicate solidarity, offering reassurance and letting others know that they are not alone in their journey. By using language that acknowledges the strength and resilience of individuals, we empower them to embrace their own agency and move forward on a path of personal transformation. Through the power of language, we can create a community that uplifts, supports, and inspires, providing a foundation for individuals to reclaim their narratives, find their voice, and forge new paths beyond the confines of victimhood.

The relationship between language, self-perception, and the ability to overcome adversity is profound. The words we use to describe ourselves and our experiences have a profound impact on how we perceive ourselves and navigate challenges. When we adopt a language of resilience, strength, and growth, we cultivate a mindset that enables us to face adversity with determination and optimism. By reframing our narratives and using empowering language, we can shift from a victim mentality to a mindset of personal agency and empowerment. Our choice of words can shape our self-perception, influencing how we interpret and respond to setbacks and obstacles. When we use language that acknowledges our capacity to overcome adversity, we strengthen our belief in our own resilience and ability to triumph. By harnessing the power of language, we can transform our perception of ourselves and our circumstances, allowing us to rise above challenges and embrace a mindset of possibility and triumph.

The potential for empowerment through language is immense, as it has the ability to create opportunities for resilience and personal growth. The words we choose to use, both in our self-talk and in our interactions with others, shape our thoughts, beliefs, and actions. By intentionally employing language that fosters empowerment, we can cultivate a mindset that embraces challenges as opportunities for growth. Empowering language encourages us to see setbacks as temporary obstacles and to view ourselves as capable and resilient individuals. It inspires us to take ownership of our experiences and to seek out solutions rather than dwell on limitations. Through the power of language, we can reframe our narratives, shifting from victimhood to empowerment. By embracing empowering words and affirmations, we open ourselves up to new possibilities and the realization of our full potential. Language becomes a catalyst for personal transformation, creating a supportive environment that nurtures resilience, fosters personal growth, and empowers us to navigate life's challenges with strength and determination.

Language holds the power to empower individuals to define their own identities and narratives, free from the confines of victimhood. It provides a platform for individuals to reclaim their agency and assert their own truths. By using language intentionally, individuals can craft narratives that reflect their strengths, aspirations, and resilience. Language enables individuals to transcend societal expectations and stereotypes, offering a means to challenge and reshape limiting narratives imposed upon them. Through self-affirming language, individuals can assert their autonomy and assert their unique identities. They can redefine their stories, emphasizing their growth, accomplishments, and potential rather than being defined solely by their past experiences of victimization. By embracing empowering language, individuals not only break free from the constraints of victimhood but also cultivate a sense of self-determination, fostering a genuine and authentic expression of who they are. Language becomes a tool of empowerment, allowing individuals to shape their own narratives, reclaim their identities, and confidently navigate the world on their own terms.

Language plays a vital role in promoting proactive problem-solving approaches to challenges. The words we use shape our perception of problems and influence the strategies we employ to address them. By employing language that encourages a proactive mindset, individuals are empowered to view challenges as opportunities for growth and development. Positive and solution-focused language fosters a sense of agency and resilience, encouraging individuals to take ownership of their circumstances and seek innovative solutions. It promotes a mindset of action and resourcefulness, emphasizing the importance of taking proactive steps to overcome obstacles rather than succumbing to a victim mentality. Language that emphasizes resilience, adaptability, and creativity encourages individuals to approach challenges with a problem-solving mindset, seeking alternative perspectives, and exploring new possibilities. By harnessing the power of language, individuals can reframe their approach to challenges, viewing them as stepping stones towards personal growth and transformation.

Language plays a crucial role in fostering a sense of collective empowerment and driving social change. Through the power of words, individuals can articulate their shared experiences, express their aspirations, and advocate for justice and equality. Language acts as a unifying force, bringing people together around common goals and values. It enables the articulation of collective grievances, amplifies marginalized voices, and mobilizes communities towards transformative action. By using inclusive and empowering language, individuals can challenge oppressive systems, dismantle harmful narratives, and promote empathy and understanding. Language has the potential to inspire and motivate, instilling a sense of agency and empowerment within individuals and communities. It serves as a catalyst for dialogue, enabling the exchange of diverse perspectives and the creation of shared narratives that shape the collective consciousness. When harnessed effectively, language can spark social movements, foster solidarity, and ignite positive change. It has the power to challenge the status quo, redefine societal norms, and build a more inclusive and equitable future for all.

The power of language to reframe experiences and shift from a victim mindset to one of resilience and strength should not be underestimated. Our words have the ability to shape our perceptions and interpretations of events, influencing how we see ourselves and the world around us. By consciously choosing empowering and growth-oriented language, we can transform our narratives and redefine our experiences. Instead of dwelling on past hardships and setbacks, we can reframe them as opportunities for growth and learning. Through language, we can acknowledge the challenges we have faced while emphasizing our ability to overcome them and thrive. By shifting our focus from victimhood to resilience, we can cultivate a mindset that empowers us to face adversity with courage and determination. This reframing process allows us to recognize our inner strength, build resilience, and embrace a sense of agency and self-efficacy. Through the power of language, we can rewrite our stories, reclaim our power, and forge a path of resilience and strength.

Empowering language has the capacity to challenge and dismantle societal structures that perpetuate victimhood and marginalization. By using language that promotes inclusivity, equality, and empowerment, we can disrupt the narratives that reinforce systemic inequalities and discrimination. Empowering language allows us to challenge the dominant discourse that assigns blame and perpetuates stereotypes about certain individuals or groups. It encourages us to acknowledge and challenge the power imbalances and oppressive systems that marginalize and disempower certain communities. Through the use of empowering language, we can amplify marginalized voices, question unjust social structures, and advocate for meaningful change. By shifting the narrative and highlighting the resilience, strength, and agency of individuals and communities, empowering language becomes a powerful tool for dismantling societal barriers, promoting justice, and fostering a more inclusive and equitable society. It invites us to envision and create a world where everyone is valued, respected, and empowered to reach their fullest potential.

Language plays a vital role in breaking down barriers and promoting inclusivity for individuals who have experienced victimization. By using inclusive and empathetic language, we create a safe and supportive environment that acknowledges and validates their experiences. Through language, we can foster a sense of belonging and acceptance, allowing individuals to share their stories without fear of judgment or further victimization. Inclusive language also helps to challenge stigmatizing stereotypes and biases, allowing us to see individuals beyond their victimization and recognize their multifaceted identities. By promoting inclusivity through our words, we create opportunities for healing, empowerment, and the restoration of dignity for those who have been victimized. It is through language that we can build bridges of understanding and empathy, fostering a culture of compassion and support for survivors. By actively choosing language that uplifts and respects their experiences, we contribute to a more inclusive and equitable society that values the worth and resilience of every individual, regardless of their past victimization.

Language possesses a remarkable ability to inspire hope, motivation, and a sense of possibility in individuals who are overcoming victimhood. Through carefully chosen words and narratives, we can create a narrative that empowers and uplifts, encouraging individuals to envision a future beyond their past experiences. By using language that acknowledges their strength, resilience, and inherent worth, we help them recognize their own potential and capacity for growth. Inspirational language can serve as a catalyst for personal transformation, instilling a belief in oneself and the possibility of a brighter tomorrow. It provides a roadmap for navigating the challenges, offering encouragement and reminding individuals that their past does not define their future. By leveraging the power of language to instill hope and motivation, we enable individuals to embrace their own agency, rewrite their narratives, and forge a path towards healing and fulfillment. In this way, language becomes a powerful tool in fostering resilience, igniting determination, and inspiring individuals to reclaim their lives with a renewed sense of purpose and possibility.

In the context of trauma recovery and healing, language plays a crucial role in personal empowerment. The way we articulate our experiences and emotions can either reinforce the narrative of victimhood or empower us to reclaim our agency and identity. By using language that acknowledges the strength and resilience within us, we begin to rewrite the narrative of our trauma. Positive and empowering language can help us reframe our experiences, focusing not only on the pain and suffering but also on the journey of healing and growth. It allows us to express our emotions and thoughts with clarity, fostering a deeper understanding of our own inner world. Moreover, language enables us to communicate our needs, seek support, and engage in meaningful connections with others. Through self-compassion and empowering self-talk, we gradually build a foundation of resilience and self-empowerment. By embracing language as a tool for healing, we harness its transformative power to navigate the complexities of trauma recovery, reclaim our identities, and cultivate a renewed sense of purpose and strength.

The importance of using language that acknowledges and honors the strength and resilience of survivors cannot be overstated. Survivors of various forms of victimization have endured unimaginable challenges and demonstrated remarkable courage in their journeys of healing. By using language that recognizes their inner strength and resilience, we validate their experiences and empower them to reclaim their narratives. It is crucial to acknowledge their resilience as a testament to their spirit and their ability to persevere. By reframing their stories with words that highlight their strength, we create a space that honors their resilience and fosters a sense of empowerment. This language not only supports survivors in their healing process but also challenges societal narratives that often portray them solely as victims. By acknowledging their strength and resilience, we help create a culture that celebrates survivors and provides them with the recognition and support they deserve.

The potential for language to bridge divides and create opportunities for empathy and connection among diverse groups is immense. Language serves as a powerful tool to foster understanding, dismantle stereotypes, and promote meaningful dialogue. When we use language that is inclusive, respectful, and compassionate, we create an environment that encourages empathy and openness. By actively listening to and learning from diverse perspectives, we can broaden our understanding of the world and develop a deeper appreciation for the experiences of others. Language has the ability to humanize individuals, breaking down barriers and fostering genuine connections. It allows us to communicate our thoughts, emotions, and experiences in ways that transcend differences in background, culture, and identity. By harnessing the potential of language to promote empathy and connection, we can build bridges of understanding and create a more inclusive and compassionate society.

The role of language in shifting the narrative around victimhood from one of passivity to one of active agency is transformative. Language has the power to shape our perceptions and understanding of ourselves and the world around us. By using language that emphasizes empowerment, resilience, and personal agency, we can challenge the notion that victims are passive and helpless. Instead, we can highlight the strength and courage individuals possess in navigating and overcoming difficult circumstances. By reframing the narrative, we can inspire a mindset of active agency, where individuals reclaim their power and take charge of their own lives. Language becomes a tool for liberation, allowing individuals to see themselves as active participants in their own narratives, capable of making choices and effecting change. It encourages a sense of personal responsibility and fosters a belief in one's ability to shape their own destiny. By harnessing the power of language, we can empower individuals to break free from the confines of victimhood and embrace a narrative of strength, resilience, and active agency.

The power of language in fostering a sense of empowerment, belonging, and social support for individuals moving beyond victimhood is profound. Language has the ability to shape our perceptions and create meaningful connections with others. By using empowering and inclusive language, we can create a safe and supportive environment where individuals feel seen, heard, and validated. It is through language that we can inspire a sense of empowerment, reminding individuals of their inherent strength and resilience. By emphasizing the collective experiences and shared struggles, language can foster a sense of belonging and create a supportive community. It provides a platform for individuals to share their stories, seek guidance, and offer encouragement to others on a similar journey. The power of language lies not only in its ability to express our thoughts and emotions but also in its capacity to uplift, inspire, and unite. Through empowering language, we can build a culture that celebrates growth, resilience, and the transformative journey of moving beyond victimhood.

Language holds immense power as a catalyst for societal change, promoting empathy, and creating a more inclusive and empowering culture. The words we choose and the way we communicate can shape our collective understanding, attitudes, and behaviors. By using language that is inclusive, respectful, and affirming, we can challenge biases and stereotypes, fostering empathy and understanding among diverse individuals and communities. When we consciously choose words that promote equality and justice, we create a foundation for positive social transformation. Language becomes a tool for dismantling systemic barriers, amplifying marginalized voices, and creating spaces where everyone feels valued and heard. By embracing language as a catalyst for change, we can foster a more compassionate and inclusive society that empowers individuals to be their authentic selves, celebrates diversity, and actively works towards a more equitable future.

12. Overcoming Victim Chic: Strategies for Taking Control of Our Lives

Recognizing and challenging victim mentality is an important step towards personal growth and empowerment. Victim mentality refers to a mindset in which individuals perceive themselves as helpless and constantly at the mercy of external circumstances. It can hinder personal development, limit problem-solving abilities, and perpetuate a cycle of negativity and disempowerment. By acknowledging the influence of victim mentality in our lives, we can begin to take ownership of our experiences and choices. This involves reframing our narratives, focusing on personal agency, and adopting a proactive approach to challenges. Challenging victim mentality requires self-reflection, self-awareness, and a willingness to break free from self-limiting beliefs. It involves cultivating resilience, embracing a growth mindset, and seeking opportunities for personal empowerment. By recognizing and challenging victim mentality, we open ourselves up to new possibilities, reclaim our personal power, and create a path towards a more fulfilling and empowered life.

Practicing gratitude and focusing on what you can control are essential strategies for cultivating a positive mindset and overcoming victimhood. When we shift our attention towards gratitude, we acknowledge the blessings and positive aspects of our lives, no matter how small they may seem. This practice helps us reframe our perspective and appreciate the abundance that surrounds us. Additionally, focusing on what we can control empowers us to take proactive steps towards creating positive change. Rather than dwelling on circumstances outside our influence, we direct our energy towards actions and decisions within our reach. This shift in mindset allows us to reclaim our agency and take ownership of our lives. By practicing gratitude and focusing on what we can control, we cultivate resilience, develop a sense of empowerment, and break free from the limitations of victimhood.

Building resilience through self-care and personal growth is a powerful antidote to victimhood. Self-care involves prioritizing our physical, emotional, and mental well-being. It encompasses activities such as practicing mindfulness, engaging in regular exercise, nourishing our bodies with nutritious food, getting enough rest, and seeking support from loved ones. Taking care of ourselves equips us with the strength and energy needed to navigate life's challenges. Additionally, personal growth involves continuous learning and self-reflection. It entails seeking opportunities for personal development, setting goals, and embracing new experiences. By investing in our personal growth, we expand our skills, knowledge, and perspectives, empowering ourselves to adapt and thrive in the face of adversity. Through self-care and personal growth, we cultivate resilience, strengthen our inner resources, and develop the resilience needed to overcome obstacles and break free from the limitations of victimhood.

Seeking support from positive and empowering relationships is crucial in moving away from a victim mentality. Surrounding ourselves with individuals who uplift and encourage us can help shift our perspective and provide the necessary support to overcome challenges. These relationships can be with friends, family members, mentors, or support groups that foster a sense of belonging and understanding. They offer a safe space to express our emotions, share our experiences, and receive validation and guidance. By connecting with others who promote personal growth and empowerment, we gain fresh insights, alternative perspectives, and encouragement to challenge negative thought patterns. These supportive relationships provide a source of strength, motivation, and accountability, empowering us to take ownership of our lives and move towards a mindset of resilience and self-empowerment.

Setting achievable goals and taking action towards them is a powerful way to break free from a victim mentality. By defining clear and attainable objectives, we regain a sense of control and purpose in our lives. These goals can be small steps towards personal growth, professional development, or any area of life where we seek improvement. Setting achievable goals helps us shift our focus from feeling powerless to being proactive and intentional in our actions. It allows us to channel our energy towards positive change and progress, reinforcing our belief in our own capabilities. As we take consistent steps towards our goals, we build confidence, resilience, and a sense of accomplishment. Each small achievement becomes a testament to our ability to shape our own future, further empowering us to overcome challenges and transcend the limitations of victimhood.

Cultivating a growth mindset and embracing challenges as opportunities for learning is essential in breaking free from a victim mentality. Instead of viewing setbacks and obstacles as permanent roadblocks, a growth mindset enables us to see them as stepping stones towards personal and professional development. It encourages us to embrace challenges, knowing that they hold valuable lessons and opportunities for growth. By reframing our perception of difficulties, we shift our focus from self-pity to resilience and perseverance. We become open to new possibilities, willing to take risks, and eager to learn from our experiences. With a growth mindset, we understand that failure is not a reflection of our worth but a natural part of the learning process. It empowers us to take ownership of our journey, adapt to changing circumstances, and continuously evolve. By cultivating a growth mindset, we can transform our perspective on challenges and break free from the limitations of victimhood.

Engaging in activities that promote empowerment and agency is a crucial step towards breaking free from a victim mentality. By actively participating in activities that align with our passions, values, and goals, we regain a sense of control and autonomy over our lives. These activities can vary widely, from pursuing hobbies and interests that bring us joy to taking on new challenges that stretch our capabilities. Engaging in meaningful work, volunteering, or advocating for causes we believe in can also foster a sense of purpose and empowerment. By proactively seeking out opportunities to make a positive impact and contribute to our communities, we regain a sense of agency and influence over our circumstances. Additionally, practicing self-care, setting boundaries, and prioritizing our well-being are vital aspects of empowering ourselves. By engaging in activities that promote empowerment and agency, we reclaim our power, discover our strengths, and take proactive steps towards creating a fulfilling and meaningful life.

Reframing negative thoughts and self-talk is a powerful tool for breaking free from a victim mentality. Our thoughts shape our perceptions, emotions, and actions, so it is essential to consciously challenge and reframe negative patterns of thinking. Instead of dwelling on self-limiting beliefs or engaging in self-defeating thoughts, we can actively replace them with more positive and empowering ones. This involves recognizing negative thought patterns, questioning their validity, and consciously replacing them with more constructive and affirming thoughts. By reframing negative thoughts, we can cultivate a mindset of resilience, self-compassion, and self-belief. This shift in thinking allows us to see challenges as opportunities for growth, setbacks as temporary hurdles, and ourselves as capable and deserving of success. Reframing negative thoughts and self-talk empowers us to take control of our internal narrative, fostering a mindset that supports our well-being, personal growth, and overall empowerment.

Learning to assert boundaries and communicate effectively is a vital aspect of personal empowerment. Setting boundaries allows us to define and protect our physical, emotional, and mental well-being. It involves understanding our needs, values, and limits, and then clearly communicating them to others. Effective communication plays a key role in expressing our boundaries and needs, as well as resolving conflicts and asserting ourselves respectfully. By developing assertiveness skills, we can express our thoughts, feelings, and boundaries in a confident and respectful manner, without compromising our values or allowing others to infringe upon our rights. Learning to assert boundaries and communicate effectively empowers us to advocate for ourselves, maintain healthy relationships, and navigate various situations with confidence and assertiveness. It is an essential skill that contributes to our overall well-being and personal growth.

Taking responsibility for our emotions and reactions is an important aspect of personal growth and empowerment. It involves recognizing that we have control over how we respond to situations and that our emotions are influenced by our own thoughts, beliefs, and perspectives. By acknowledging our emotional responses, we can gain insight into ourselves and develop a greater understanding of our triggers and patterns. Taking responsibility means not blaming others for how we feel but instead recognizing that our reactions are within our own power to manage. It involves practicing self-awareness, mindfulness, and emotional regulation techniques to navigate challenging situations in a constructive and healthy way. When we take responsibility for our emotions and reactions, we empower ourselves to make conscious choices and respond in a manner that aligns with our values and goals. It allows us to cultivate emotional resilience, maintain healthier relationships, and create a more fulfilling and empowered life.

Developing a sense of purpose and meaning beyond victimhood is a transformative step towards personal empowerment and growth. It involves recognizing that our identity is not defined solely by our past experiences or the challenges we have faced. By exploring our passions, values, and interests, we can tap into a deeper sense of purpose that extends beyond being a victim. This shift in perspective allows us to reclaim our agency and create a narrative that emphasizes our strengths, resilience, and capacity for growth. Developing a sense of purpose provides us with a guiding compass, driving us to pursue meaningful goals and make a positive impact in our own lives and the lives of others. It allows us to shift our focus from dwelling on past victimization to actively shaping our future with intention and determination. By embracing a sense of purpose, we can transcend victimhood and embark on a path of personal fulfillment, empowerment, and contribution to the world around us.

Practicing forgiveness and letting go of resentment is a powerful act of self-liberation and personal growth. Holding onto grudges and resentments only keeps us tied to the past, prolonging our victimhood and preventing us from moving forward. By choosing to forgive, we free ourselves from the emotional burden and negative energy that resentment carries. Forgiveness does not mean condoning or forgetting the harm inflicted upon us, but rather, it is a conscious decision to release ourselves from the grip of bitterness and anger. It allows us to reclaim our power and control over our own emotions and responses. Through forgiveness, we can break free from the cycle of victimhood and open ourselves up to healing, inner peace, and the possibility of building healthier relationships. By practicing forgiveness, we create space for growth, personal transformation, and the cultivation of empathy and understanding.

Recognizing the power of choice is a transformative realization that empowers individuals to take control of their lives. In every situation, we have the power to choose our attitude, actions, and responses. While we may not have control over external circumstances, we have the ability to determine how we interpret and navigate them. Understanding that our choices shape our experiences, relationships, and overall well-being allows us to step out of the victim mindset and embrace a proactive and empowered approach to life. By recognizing the power of choice, we can actively pursue our goals, make positive changes, and overcome challenges. We can choose to prioritize our values, invest in personal growth, and surround ourselves with supportive influences. Each choice we make is an opportunity to shape our present and future, and by harnessing this power, we can create a life aligned with our aspirations and values.

Focusing on our strengths and building upon them is a powerful strategy for personal growth and empowerment. Each of us possesses unique talents, skills, and qualities that contribute to our individuality and potential. By directing our attention to these strengths, we can cultivate a sense of self-confidence and competence. Rather than fixating on our perceived limitations or dwelling on areas of weakness, we can channel our energy towards developing and enhancing our strengths. This intentional focus allows us to capitalize on our natural abilities and talents, leveraging them to overcome obstacles and seize opportunities. Embracing our strengths also nurtures a positive self-image and helps us to recognize our inherent value and worth. By continually building upon our strengths, we can expand our capabilities, achieve personal goals, and cultivate a greater sense of self-efficacy.

Taking ownership of our mistakes is an essential part of personal growth and development. It requires humility, self-reflection, and a willingness to acknowledge when we have made errors or caused harm. By taking responsibility for our actions, we demonstrate accountability and integrity.

Rather than deflecting blame or making excuses, we confront the consequences of our mistakes and make a genuine effort to learn from them. This process of self-examination and learning allows us to gain valuable insights into our behaviors, beliefs, and values. It empowers us to make positive changes, develop healthier habits, and cultivate greater self-awareness. By embracing our mistakes as opportunities for growth and transformation, we can not only avoid repeating them but also deepen our understanding of ourselves and others. Taking ownership of our mistakes fosters personal responsibility, promotes continuous learning, and enables us to become more compassionate, empathetic individuals.

Avoiding the habit of blaming others for our problems is a crucial step towards personal growth and self-empowerment. It requires taking ownership of our circumstances and recognizing that we have agency in shaping our lives. Blaming others may provide temporary relief by shifting responsibility away from ourselves, but it ultimately hinders our ability to find solutions and create positive change. By acknowledging our role in the situations we face, we gain the power to evaluate our choices, attitudes, and actions. We can then identify areas for improvement and make conscious decisions to overcome challenges. Embracing personal accountability enables us to approach difficulties with a proactive mindset, seeking solutions rather than dwelling on grievances. It empowers us to adopt a problem-solving attitude and take the necessary steps to create the outcomes we desire. By avoiding the tendency to blame others, we can cultivate resilience, self-reliance, and a greater sense of personal agency in navigating life's challenges.

Finding meaning in adversity can be a transformative experience that propels personal growth and resilience. When faced with challenging circumstances, it is natural to feel overwhelmed and disheartened. However, by reframing adversity as an opportunity for growth, we can shift our perspective and find purpose in our experiences. Adversity often presents valuable lessons, pushing us to explore our strengths, values, and priorities. It prompts us to reflect on our lives, question our assumptions, and discover untapped potential. By embracing adversity as a catalyst for growth, we can develop a deeper understanding of ourselves and the world around us. It encourages us to seek new perspectives, adopt a growth mindset, and explore innovative solutions to overcome obstacles. Furthermore, finding meaning in adversity can inspire empathy and compassion for others who face similar challenges, fostering connection and a sense of shared humanity. Ultimately, by using adversity as a catalyst for growth, we can transform our lives, cultivate resilience, and create a meaningful and fulfilling existence.

Embracing discomfort and challenging oneself to step outside of the comfort zone is a powerful pathway to personal growth and empowerment. It is easy to become complacent and settle into familiar routines and situations that feel safe and predictable. However, true growth occurs when we push ourselves beyond our comfort limits and confront the unknown. By willingly embracing discomfort, we open ourselves to new experiences, opportunities, and perspectives that can expand our horizons and reshape our understanding of what is possible. Stepping outside of our comfort zone allows us to develop resilience, adaptability, and confidence in navigating unfamiliar territory. It enables us to overcome fears, break through self-imposed limitations, and discover hidden strengths and capabilities. While discomfort may initially feel challenging, it often serves as a catalyst for personal transformation, fostering resilience and equipping us with the tools to tackle future obstacles with greater confidence. Embracing discomfort is a courageous choice that invites growth, self-discovery, and a richer, more fulfilling life.

Taking a proactive approach to problem-solving is an empowering mindset that allows individuals to tackle challenges head-on and take control of their circumstances. Rather than passively accepting problems as insurmountable obstacles, a proactive mindset encourages individuals to actively seek solutions and take responsibility for finding them. It involves recognizing that problems are opportunities for growth and learning, and that there are often multiple paths to resolution. By taking the initiative to identify and address issues, individuals can avoid being overwhelmed or paralyzed by them. A proactive approach involves being proactive rather than reactive, anticipating potential challenges, and developing strategies to mitigate them. It requires clear communication, collaboration, and a willingness to explore creative and innovative solutions. Embracing a proactive problem-solving mindset empowers individuals to be agents of change in their own lives, enabling them to navigate obstacles with confidence and resilience.

Recognizing and challenging negative self-talk and limiting beliefs is a crucial step towards personal growth and empowerment. Negative self-talk refers to the inner dialogue that often consists of self-criticism, doubt, and self-limiting beliefs. These thoughts can undermine our confidence, hinder our progress, and reinforce a victim mentality. By becoming aware of these negative patterns of thinking, we can consciously challenge and replace them with more positive and empowering thoughts. This involves questioning the validity and accuracy of our negative self-perceptions, reframing our self-talk in a more compassionate and supportive manner, and focusing on our strengths and accomplishments. Challenging limiting beliefs entails examining the beliefs we hold about ourselves and the world, and actively challenging those that are holding us back. It requires questioning the evidence and rationality behind these beliefs, seeking alternative perspectives, and embracing a growth mindset that acknowledges our capacity for change and development. By recognizing and challenging negative self-talk and limiting beliefs, we can cultivate a more empowering and optimistic mindset that fuels personal growth and resilience.

Learning to differentiate between being a victim and being victimized is a crucial step in reclaiming personal power and promoting a sense of agency. Being a victim implies a state of helplessness and passivity, where one perceives themselves as being constantly at the mercy of external circumstances. On the other hand, being victimized refers to experiencing harm, injustice, or mistreatment at the hands of others or challenging situations. By recognizing this distinction, we can shift our perspective and take ownership of our response to adversity. While we may have experienced victimization, we can choose to embrace a mindset of resilience, growth, and empowerment. This involves acknowledging the impact of the past but refusing to let it define our present and future. By focusing on our strengths, building healthy boundaries, seeking support, and taking proactive steps towards healing and growth, we can transcend the role of a victim and become agents of our own lives. Differentiating between being a victim and being victimized allows us to break free from the disempowering mindset of victimhood and embrace a more empowered and proactive approach to life's challenges.

Practicing empathy towards others while maintaining personal responsibility is an essential skill in fostering healthy relationships and promoting understanding. Empathy involves the ability to put ourselves in someone else's shoes, to understand their emotions, perspectives, and experiences. It allows us to connect with others on a deeper level and cultivate compassion. However, practicing empathy does not mean absolving others of their responsibilities or neglecting our own. It means recognizing and acknowledging the emotions and struggles of others while still holding them accountable for their actions. It involves setting healthy boundaries, communicating our needs and expectations, and encouraging personal growth and accountability. By striking a balance between empathy and personal responsibility, we can create a supportive and compassionate environment where individuals are both understood and encouraged to take ownership of their actions and choices.

13. The Importance of Boundaries: Setting Limits and Protecting Our Well-Being

Boundaries play a crucial role in safeguarding our mental and emotional well-being. They serve as protective barriers that define what is acceptable and what is not in our relationships, interactions, and personal lives. Setting clear boundaries allows us to establish our limits, protect our time and energy, and prioritize self-care. By communicating our boundaries, we create a safe and respectful space where our needs and values are honored. Boundaries help prevent emotional exhaustion, burnout, and resentment by ensuring that we maintain a healthy balance between giving and receiving. They empower us to say no when necessary, assert our preferences, and protect ourselves from toxic or harmful situations. Establishing and maintaining boundaries is an act of self-care and self-respect, enabling us to cultivate healthier relationships and maintain a positive sense of well-being.

Setting and enforcing boundaries is an essential practice that can significantly contribute to preventing burnout and reducing stress. When we establish clear boundaries, we define our limits and communicate them to others, allowing us to protect our time, energy, and overall well-being. By setting boundaries around our work hours, personal commitments, and social interactions, we create a healthy balance between our responsibilities and personal needs. This helps prevent the overwhelming feeling of being constantly available and accommodating to others' demands. By enforcing these boundaries, we prioritize self-care and ensure that we have the time and space to recharge and rejuvenate. This proactive approach allows us to manage our stress levels effectively, prevent burnout, and maintain a healthier and more sustainable lifestyle. By setting and enforcing boundaries, we empower ourselves to make our well-being a priority and create a more balanced and fulfilling life.

Establishing clear boundaries can have a transformative impact on our relationships with others. By clearly defining our needs, limits, and expectations, we create a foundation of mutual respect and understanding. Boundaries provide a framework for healthy and balanced interactions, enabling us to communicate our preferences and priorities effectively. They help us avoid situations where our boundaries are violated or compromised, leading to resentment or conflict. By setting boundaries, we teach others how to treat us and create space for open and honest communication. This fosters a sense of trust and safety within our relationships, as both parties know where the lines are drawn and what is expected. Clear boundaries also promote accountability and responsibility, as each individual is aware of their role in maintaining the agreed-upon boundaries. Ultimately, by establishing and respecting boundaries, we cultivate healthier and more fulfilling relationships built on mutual respect, understanding, and support.

Boundaries play a crucial role in helping us prioritize our own needs and goals. By setting clear boundaries, we create a framework that allows us to allocate our time, energy, and resources in alignment with our personal well-being and aspirations. Boundaries enable us to establish healthy limits on what we can and cannot take on, ensuring that we avoid overextending ourselves or becoming overwhelmed. They provide us with the necessary space and time to focus on self-care, personal growth, and the pursuit of our goals. By honoring our boundaries, we send a powerful message to ourselves and others that our needs and aspirations matter. This allows us to make intentional choices about how we invest our time and energy, ensuring that we prioritize what truly aligns with our values and aspirations. Boundaries provide the necessary structure to maintain balance and prevent burnout, empowering us to lead more fulfilling and purposeful lives.

Saying "no" and setting limits is an essential aspect of self-care. It allows us to prioritize our own well-being and ensure that our resources, including time, energy, and emotional capacity, are utilized in a way that serves us best. By recognizing our own limits and honoring them through setting boundaries, we create space for rest, rejuvenation, and the pursuit of activities that nourish us. Saying "no" is not a selfish act; rather, it is an act of self-respect and self-preservation. It enables us to avoid overcommitment, burnout, and resentment, and it empowers us to make choices that align with our values and needs. Setting limits establishes a healthy balance between giving and receiving, allowing us to maintain our physical and emotional well-being. By prioritizing self-care through the practice of saying "no" and setting limits, we demonstrate compassion and respect for ourselves, which ultimately enhances our overall quality of life.

Setting boundaries is a powerful tool for protecting ourselves from being taken advantage of or manipulated by others. When we establish clear limits and communicate them assertively, we send a message that our needs, emotions, and personal space are valuable and deserve respect. Boundaries serve as a line of defense against those who may try to exploit our kindness, infringe upon our time and energy, or manipulate us for their own gain. By setting boundaries, we establish a framework of expectations that fosters healthy relationships built on mutual respect and reciprocity. We cultivate a sense of self-worth and self-respect, recognizing that we have the right to say no and to protect our well-being. Setting boundaries helps us preserve our autonomy and prevent the erosion of our personal boundaries, enabling us to navigate interpersonal dynamics with greater confidence and integrity. It allows us to create a safe and empowering environment where we are less susceptible to manipulation and more capable of maintaining our emotional and mental well-being.

Boundaries play a crucial role in maintaining a sense of control and agency in our lives. When we establish and enforce boundaries, we create a clear framework that defines our personal limits, values, and priorities. By doing so, we gain a greater sense of control over our time, energy, and resources. Boundaries empower us to make intentional choices about how we spend our time and with whom we engage in various aspects of our lives. They enable us to set realistic expectations, manage our commitments, and honor our own needs and desires. By respecting our boundaries, we assert our agency and demonstrate to ourselves and others that we have the power to make decisions that align with our values and well-being. Boundaries provide a sense of structure and stability, allowing us to navigate life with intentionality and maintain a healthy balance between our own needs and the demands of the outside world. Ultimately, boundaries are a fundamental tool for cultivating a sense of control, agency, and self-determination in our lives.

Clear boundaries play a pivotal role in fostering respect and mutual understanding within our relationships. When we communicate our boundaries effectively, we provide others with a clear understanding of our limits, expectations, and needs. This clarity promotes open and honest communication, allowing for a deeper level of mutual understanding and empathy. By expressing our boundaries, we establish a foundation of respect where both parties recognize and honor each other's boundaries. This mutual respect strengthens the trust and connection in our relationships, as we feel heard, valued, and understood. Clear boundaries also prevent misunderstandings and conflicts by setting clear guidelines for acceptable behavior and interactions. They create a safe and respectful space where both individuals can express themselves authentically without fear of crossing each other's boundaries. Ultimately, clear boundaries promote healthier and more fulfilling relationships based on trust, understanding, and mutual respect.

Setting boundaries can be a powerful tool in overcoming feelings of guilt and obligation. Often, we find ourselves saying "yes" to others' requests out of a sense of duty or fear of disappointing them. However, by clearly defining our limits and communicating them assertively, we reclaim our right to prioritize our own needs and well-being. This act of self-care not only helps us establish healthier boundaries but also empowers us to prioritize our own happiness and fulfillment. It allows us to let go of the guilt that may have accompanied our previous inability to say "no" and frees us from the weight of unwarranted obligations. By setting boundaries, we create space for ourselves to grow, thrive, and cultivate relationships that are based on mutual respect and understanding.

Boundaries play a crucial role in establishing and maintaining healthy communication patterns. They serve as guidelines for how we want to be treated and how we want to engage with others. By clearly expressing our needs, expectations, and limits, we create a safe space for open and honest communication. Boundaries help prevent misunderstandings, conflicts, and resentments by setting the framework for respectful and considerate interactions. They allow us to express ourselves authentically and assertively, while also encouraging others to do the same. With well-defined boundaries, we can engage in conversations that are constructive, supportive, and conducive to building stronger connections. Boundaries not only foster healthier communication but also promote trust, mutual understanding, and the development of deeper and more meaningful relationships.

Boundaries serve as essential safeguards that protect us from being overwhelmed by the demands of others. They create a clear distinction between our own needs and priorities and those of others. By setting boundaries, we establish limits on how much time, energy, and resources we are willing to allocate to different people and situations. This empowers us to prioritize our well-being and ensure that we have enough space and resources for self-care, personal growth, and pursuing our own goals. Boundaries enable us to respectfully say "no" when necessary and avoid taking on responsibilities or obligations that exceed our capacity. They provide a sense of balance and control, allowing us to maintain our own emotional and mental well-being even in the face of external pressures. By maintaining healthy boundaries, we can navigate our relationships and commitments with a greater sense of self-awareness, self-care, and personal fulfillment.

Enforcing boundaries is a crucial step in safeguarding ourselves from toxic or abusive relationships. Boundaries serve as protective barriers that define what behavior is acceptable and what is not. By clearly communicating and upholding our boundaries, we establish a framework of respect and accountability within our relationships. This empowers us to recognize and address any behaviors that violate our boundaries, such as manipulation, control, or emotional abuse. Enforcing boundaries allows us to assert our autonomy and protect our emotional, physical, and mental well-being. It enables us to create a space where healthy and nurturing relationships can thrive, while deterring harmful dynamics from taking hold. By setting and enforcing boundaries, we assert our self-worth and send a powerful message that our well-being and dignity are non-negotiable. It empowers us to surround ourselves with individuals who respect and honor our boundaries, fostering relationships that are built on trust, equality, and mutual support.

Setting boundaries serves as a compass that keeps us aligned with our values and beliefs. When we establish clear boundaries, we define what is acceptable and unacceptable based on our core principles. This empowers us to stay true to ourselves and make choices that are in harmony with our authentic selves. By setting boundaries around our values, we create a space where we can uphold our beliefs and live according to our moral compass. It allows us to protect our integrity and maintain a sense of congruence between our actions and our values. Setting boundaries based on our values also helps us navigate situations and relationships that may challenge or compromise our principles. It enables us to make decisions and engage in behaviors that are consistent with our beliefs, fostering a sense of personal fulfillment and inner alignment. By setting boundaries that honor our values and beliefs, we cultivate a life that is authentic, purposeful, and reflective of who we truly are.

Setting and maintaining boundaries is crucial for establishing a strong sense of self-worth and self-respect. By clearly defining our limits and communicating them to others, we demonstrate that we value ourselves and our well-being. Boundaries act as a protective shield, safeguarding our emotional and mental health. They enable us to prioritize our needs, desires, and values, ensuring that we engage in relationships and situations that align with our authentic selves. When we establish boundaries, we assert our worthiness of respect, kindness, and consideration from others. By respecting our own boundaries, we cultivate a deep sense of self-esteem and reinforce the belief that we deserve to be treated with dignity and fairness. Boundaries empower us to establish healthy boundaries within ourselves, allowing us to make choices that align with our values and contribute to our personal growth and happiness.

The ability to set and maintain boundaries is an essential life skill that has far-reaching benefits in various aspects of our lives. Whether it's in our personal relationships, professional settings, or even within ourselves, boundaries play a crucial role in ensuring our well-being and promoting healthy interactions. By setting clear boundaries, we establish guidelines for how we want to be treated and what we are willing to accept in our lives. This helps us maintain a sense of control and agency over our experiences and allows us to protect our physical, emotional, and mental health. Setting boundaries also enables us to communicate our needs, desires, and limits effectively, fostering healthier and more fulfilling relationships. It helps us establish mutual respect, promote understanding, and prevent misunderstandings or conflicts. Moreover, boundaries allow us to manage our time, energy, and resources effectively, preventing burnout and prioritizing our own well-being. Overall, mastering the skill of setting and maintaining boundaries empowers us to create a balanced and fulfilling life, where we can thrive while respecting ourselves and others.

14. The Value of Resilience: Cultivating Strength and Adaptability in the Face of Adversity

Resilience is a remarkable human quality that enables individuals to navigate through life's challenges and adversities with remarkable strength and adaptability. It is the ability to withstand setbacks, overcome obstacles, and bounce back from difficult experiences with renewed determination. Resilient individuals possess a unique capacity to maintain a positive mindset, learn from failures, and grow stronger in the face of adversity. They exhibit emotional intelligence, embracing their emotions and effectively managing stress and anxiety. Resilience is not about avoiding hardships or denying the pain they bring, but rather about harnessing inner strength and utilizing support systems to overcome them. It involves cultivating a growth mindset, focusing on solutions rather than dwelling on problems, and embracing change as an opportunity for personal growth. Resilience is a dynamic process that can be developed and strengthened through self-reflection, building a support network, and acquiring coping strategies. By nurturing resilience, individuals can face life's challenges with courage, resilience, and a belief in their ability to thrive even in the face of adversity.

Resilience is not an innate trait but rather a learned skill that can be cultivated and strengthened with practice and experience. It involves developing a set of adaptive strategies and behaviors that enable individuals to cope with and overcome challenges. Just as a muscle grows stronger with exercise, resilience can be developed through intentional effort and a willingness to face difficult situations head-on. It involves developing a positive mindset, fostering self-awareness, and building emotional intelligence. By actively seeking opportunities to challenge themselves, individuals can gradually build their resilience by learning from setbacks, developing problem-solving skills, and nurturing a sense of self-efficacy. Resilience is a continuous process of growth and development, and by recognizing its importance and investing in its cultivation, individuals can navigate life's ups and downs with greater confidence, flexibility, and inner strength.

Cultivating resilience goes hand in hand with developing a growth mindset, which involves embracing challenges as opportunities for learning and growth rather than as obstacles to be avoided. Resilient individuals view setbacks and failures as temporary and see them as valuable experiences that provide insights and lessons. They approach challenges with a sense of curiosity and open-mindedness, seeking to understand what went wrong and how they can improve. By reframing challenges in this way, individuals can shift their perspective and focus on finding creative solutions, building new skills, and adapting their approach. This mindset empowers individuals to persevere in the face of adversity, bounce back from setbacks, and approach future challenges with a sense of optimism and resilience. By embracing a growth mindset, individuals can cultivate resilience and harness the transformative power of challenges for personal development and success.

Resilient individuals possess a set of skills and qualities that enable them to effectively navigate and cope with stress and adversity. They have a heightened ability to regulate their emotions, manage stress, and maintain a sense of calm amidst chaos. This emotional stability allows them to make rational decisions and maintain a clear focus on their goals, even in challenging situations. Additionally, resilient individuals possess strong problem-solving and decision-making skills, which enable them to find creative solutions and adapt to changing circumstances. In the professional realm, resilience equips individuals with the ability to handle work-related pressures, setbacks, and conflicts with composure and resilience. They are more likely to bounce back from setbacks, learn from failures, and leverage their experiences to fuel personal and professional growth. Overall, resilience acts as a protective shield, empowering individuals to navigate the ups and downs of life with strength, flexibility, and a greater sense of well-being.

The benefits of resilience extend beyond the ability to cope with challenges and adversity. Research has consistently shown that resilient individuals experience improved mental health and overall well-being. They exhibit lower rates of depression, anxiety, and stress-related disorders, and have a greater sense of life satisfaction and fulfillment. Resilience also plays a significant role in the workplace, as it is closely linked to increased job satisfaction and productivity. Resilient individuals are more likely to maintain a positive attitude, persevere in the face of setbacks, and demonstrate a higher level of engagement and commitment to their work. They are better equipped to handle workplace stressors and can effectively manage work-life balance, leading to greater job satisfaction and a reduced risk of burnout. Moreover, the ability to bounce back from challenges and setbacks fosters a sense of self-efficacy and confidence, enabling individuals to take on new opportunities and achieve their goals with a greater sense of purpose and motivation.

Developing resilience is not a solitary endeavor; it thrives in the presence of strong support networks and positive relationships. Social connections and meaningful interactions play a vital role in bolstering our ability to cope with adversity. Building and nurturing relationships with family, friends, colleagues, and mentors can provide a sense of belonging, understanding, and encouragement during difficult times. These relationships serve as sources of emotional support, offering a safe space for expressing feelings, seeking guidance, and gaining perspective. Additionally, being part of a supportive community can offer opportunities for shared experiences, learning from others' resilience, and accessing valuable resources. Engaging in collaborative problem-solving, receiving constructive feedback, and offering mutual support can all contribute to the development of resilience. By surrounding ourselves with individuals who uplift and inspire us, we can cultivate resilience together and foster a sense of collective strength and empowerment.

Resilience plays a critical role in the process of coping with and recovering from traumatic experiences, such as abuse or trauma. Resilient individuals possess the inner strength and adaptive capacity to face the emotional, psychological, and physical challenges that arise in the aftermath of trauma. They exhibit a remarkable ability to navigate the complex and often overwhelming emotions associated with traumatic events, allowing them to gradually heal and regain a sense of stability and well-being. While trauma can have long-lasting effects, resilience enables individuals to tap into their inner resources and seek the support necessary for their recovery journey. Resilience empowers survivors to develop effective coping strategies, rebuild their lives, and reclaim a sense of control and agency. It is through the cultivation of resilience that survivors can gradually transform their experiences into sources of strength, wisdom, and personal growth.

Building resilience involves various strategies, including the development of a sense of purpose or meaning in life. When individuals have a clear sense of purpose, it provides them with direction, motivation, and a sense of fulfillment, which can significantly contribute to their resilience. Additionally, setting achievable goals and taking action towards them plays a crucial role in building resilience. By breaking down larger goals into smaller, manageable steps, individuals can experience a sense of progress and accomplishment, which boosts their confidence and resilience. This process encourages individuals to focus on what they can control and take proactive measures to overcome challenges and setbacks. Building resilience through purpose and goal-setting empowers individuals to navigate adversity with determination and resilience, ultimately fostering their ability to bounce back stronger in the face of future obstacles.

Resilience encompasses a fundamental aspect of personal accountability, where individuals take ownership of their thoughts, emotions, and actions. Rather than attributing their problems solely to external factors or circumstances, resilient individuals recognize the role they play in shaping their experiences and outcomes. By taking responsibility, individuals empower themselves to actively respond to challenges and setbacks, seeking solutions and learning from their experiences. This mindset shift allows them to cultivate a sense of agency and control over their lives, enabling them to navigate adversity with resilience and adaptability. Embracing personal responsibility fosters a proactive approach to problem-solving, as individuals focus on what they can change and influence, rather than dwelling on what is beyond their control. This self-empowered perspective fuels resilience, as individuals build the confidence and inner strength needed to overcome obstacles and thrive in the face of adversity.

Cultivating resilience requires prioritizing self-care and self-compassion as essential components of overall well-being. Engaging in regular exercise, getting enough sleep, and practicing mindfulness are vital practices that support mental, emotional, and physical resilience. Exercise helps release endorphins, reduces stress, and boosts energy levels, enhancing overall resilience. Adequate sleep allows the body and mind to rejuvenate, promoting mental clarity and emotional stability. Mindfulness practices, such as meditation or deep breathing exercises, cultivate present-moment awareness, reduce anxiety, and foster emotional resilience. Nurturing oneself with self-care activities not only replenishes energy but also provides a sense of balance and rejuvenation, enabling individuals to better navigate challenges and bounce back from adversity. By embracing self-compassion, individuals extend understanding, kindness, and acceptance to themselves, allowing for resilience to flourish in the face of setbacks or difficult circumstances. This practice helps counter self-criticism and promotes a mindset of growth, fostering resilience by nurturing a strong foundation of self-support and well-being.

Resilience is not solely innate; it can be cultivated and strengthened through intentional exposure to challenges and adversity. Stepping outside of one's comfort zone and actively seeking new experiences or goals that push the boundaries of personal limitations can contribute to the development of resilience. By willingly taking on new challenges, individuals expand their comfort zones, build confidence in their abilities, and develop a mindset that embraces growth and adaptability. Each encounter with adversity provides an opportunity to learn, problem-solve, and develop effective coping strategies. By actively engaging in activities that challenge and stretch one's abilities, individuals not only enhance their capacity to navigate difficult situations but also foster a sense of confidence and self-efficacy that reinforces resilience. It is through these experiences that individuals gain a deeper understanding of their own strengths, learn to persevere in the face of obstacles, and develop the resilience needed to thrive in the ever-changing landscape of life.

Resilience is not about being impervious to adversity or suppressing negative emotions; rather, it is a dynamic process of adapting and recovering from setbacks. Resilient individuals recognize that setbacks and challenges are a normal part of life and understand that experiencing negative emotions is a natural response. They do not deny or avoid their emotions, but instead learn to navigate and manage them in healthy ways. Resilience involves developing effective coping mechanisms, seeking support when needed, and maintaining a positive outlook even in the face of adversity. It is about finding the inner strength to bounce back, learn from experiences, and continue moving forward despite setbacks. Resilience is a continuous journey of growth and self-discovery, where individuals build upon their strengths, cultivate self-compassion, and embrace the inherent potential for change and renewal. By developing resilience, individuals are better equipped to face the challenges of life with courage, adaptability, and a sense of hope for the future.

Therapy or counseling can be instrumental in strengthening resilience, especially when utilizing evidence-based approaches like cognitive-behavioral therapy (CBT). CBT focuses on identifying and challenging negative thought patterns and beliefs, developing healthier coping strategies, and building resilience skills. By working with a trained therapist, individuals can gain a deeper understanding of their emotions, thoughts, and behaviors, and learn practical techniques to navigate challenges more effectively. Therapy provides a safe and supportive space to explore past experiences, process emotions, and develop new perspectives and skills. It can also offer valuable tools for managing stress, building self-esteem, and fostering positive relationships. Through therapy, individuals can develop a stronger sense of self-awareness, self-compassion, and problem-solving abilities, ultimately empowering them to overcome obstacles, build resilience, and lead more fulfilling lives.

Resilience encompasses the ability to maintain a sense of optimism and hopefulness, even when confronted with adversity and uncertainty. It involves cultivating a positive mindset that believes in the possibility of better outcomes and the capacity to navigate challenges effectively. This doesn't mean ignoring or denying the difficulties at hand, but rather adopting a proactive and solution-oriented approach. Resilient individuals understand that setbacks are temporary and view them as opportunities for growth and learning. They maintain an optimistic outlook, focusing on strengths, resources, and potential solutions. This optimistic mindset provides the motivation and resilience needed to persevere through tough times, find meaning in difficult experiences, and ultimately emerge stronger on the other side. It enables individuals to adapt, find creative solutions, and maintain hope even in the face of adversity, fostering their ability to bounce back and thrive in the long run.

Building resilience involves learning from past experiences and using them as valuable opportunities for growth and development. It entails reflecting on challenging situations and identifying the lessons they offer. Resilient individuals view setbacks as stepping stones rather than stumbling blocks, understanding that each experience presents a chance to learn, adapt, and become stronger. They actively seek to gain insights from their past, examining how they responded to adversity, what strategies worked or didn't work, and how they can apply those lessons moving forward. By embracing a growth mindset and reframing setbacks as valuable learning experiences, individuals can cultivate resilience and develop the skills needed to navigate future challenges with greater strength and wisdom. This continuous process of self-reflection and learning allows individuals to build upon their experiences, refine their coping mechanisms, and ultimately foster their resilience in the face of adversity.

Resilience involves developing a sense of self-efficacy and a steadfast belief in one's ability to overcome challenges and achieve goals. It is the deep-rooted confidence that arises from acknowledging and leveraging one's strengths, skills, and resources. Resilient individuals cultivate a positive mindset that fuels their motivation and determination to persevere, even in the face of obstacles or setbacks. They understand that they have the power to influence the outcome of their lives and actively seek opportunities to demonstrate their competence and capacity for growth. Through intentional efforts and consistent practice, they build a strong foundation of self-belief, which serves as a guiding force during difficult times. This sense of self-efficacy empowers individuals to face challenges head-on, take calculated risks, and remain resilient in the pursuit of their goals. By nurturing and reinforcing this belief in their own capabilities, individuals can cultivate a resilient mindset that propels them towards success and fulfillment.

Resilient individuals possess a remarkable ability to manage their emotions and maintain a positive outlook, even during the most challenging times. They possess a heightened awareness of their emotions and have developed effective strategies for regulating and expressing them constructively. Rather than being overwhelmed by negative emotions, they harness their inner strength and resilience to navigate through adversity with grace and composure. They understand that emotions are temporary and do not define their overall well-being. With an optimistic mindset, they actively seek out silver linings, learning opportunities, and reasons for gratitude in the midst of difficult circumstances. This positive outlook fuels their resilience, enabling them to bounce back from setbacks and find the motivation to keep moving forward. By maintaining emotional balance and a positive mindset, resilient individuals effectively manage the ups and downs of life, fostering their own well-being and inspiring those around them with their unwavering strength.

Cultivating resilience often involves developing a deep sense of gratitude and appreciation for the positive aspects of life, even in the midst of challenges or adversity. Resilient individuals recognize that although difficult times may be present, there are still blessings and moments of joy to be found. They consciously shift their focus towards what they are grateful for, whether it be the support of loved ones, the beauty of nature, or personal achievements and strengths. By nurturing a gratitude practice, they become attuned to the small, meaningful moments that bring joy and fulfillment. This practice of gratitude not only helps them maintain a positive perspective but also enhances their overall well-being. It provides a foundation of resilience by reminding them of the abundance and resilience already present in their lives. Through the lens of gratitude, they find solace, inspiration, and renewed strength to face challenges head-on.

Resilience is closely intertwined with the ability to adapt and be flexible in the face of changing circumstances. Resilient individuals understand that life is filled with unexpected twists and turns, and they embrace the need to adjust their plans and strategies accordingly. They recognize that clinging rigidly to old ways of thinking or behaving can hinder their progress and hinder their ability to overcome obstacles. Instead, they cultivate a mindset of flexibility and open-mindedness, always seeking new solutions and approaches when faced with challenges. They understand that adaptability is a strength, allowing them to navigate uncertainty and change with greater ease. By embracing adaptability, they become more adept at finding alternative paths, learning from failures, and transforming setbacks into opportunities for growth. This willingness to adjust and evolve not only enhances their resilience but also empowers them to thrive in an ever-changing world.

Building resilience involves recognizing and harnessing the power of our personal strengths and resources. Resilient individuals take the time to identify their unique qualities, skills, and knowledge that can help them navigate challenges. They understand that they possess inherent strengths and capabilities that can be tapped into during difficult times. They also recognize the value of support networks, whether it be friends, family, or professional connections, and actively seek assistance when needed. By leveraging their strengths and resources, they gain a sense of empowerment and confidence in their ability to overcome adversity. They utilize their skills and knowledge to develop effective strategies and problem-solving approaches, and they rely on their support networks to provide guidance, encouragement, and assistance along the way. By recognizing and utilizing these personal assets, resilient individuals are better equipped to weather the storms of life and emerge stronger on the other side.

Resilience is not simply about passively enduring difficult circumstances; it is about taking an active role in one's own well-being. Resilient individuals understand that waiting for external factors to change is not a sustainable or effective strategy. Instead, they adopt a proactive approach, focusing on what they can control and taking deliberate actions to improve their situation. They prioritize self-care, engaging in activities that promote physical, mental, and emotional well-being. They seek out opportunities for growth and personal development, continuously learning and acquiring new skills. They set goals and take steps towards achieving them, embracing a sense of agency and personal responsibility. By taking an active role in their own well-being, resilient individuals empower themselves to navigate challenges, adapt to change, and create positive outcomes in their lives. They understand that true resilience comes from within and can be cultivated through intentional effort and self-determination.

Cultivating resilience goes beyond simply enduring adversity; it involves embracing a mindset of curiosity and openness to new experiences. Resilient individuals recognize that uncertainty and risk are inherent parts of life and instead of shying away from them, they approach them with a sense of exploration and eagerness. They view challenges as opportunities for growth and learning, seeking out new experiences that push them outside of their comfort zones. By cultivating a sense of curiosity, they remain adaptable and flexible, willing to embrace change and explore alternative paths. This mindset allows them to navigate unfamiliar territories with resilience and adaptability, discovering hidden strengths and resources along the way. Through their openness to new experiences, resilient individuals continually expand their horizons, broadening their perspectives, and developing the skills necessary to thrive in an ever-changing world.

Resilient individuals possess a remarkable ability to maintain a sense of perspective, even when faced with overwhelming challenges and stress. They recognize that amidst the chaos, it is crucial to take a step back, assess the situation, and prioritize what truly matters in their lives. They understand that not all problems are of equal significance and that their energy and focus should be directed towards what aligns with their values and long-term well-being. By maintaining perspective, they can avoid getting caught up in minor setbacks or distractions, allowing them to conserve their energy for what truly deserves their attention and effort. This sense of perspective enables them to make wise decisions, effectively manage their time and resources, and maintain a balanced perspective on both the joys and hardships of life. By prioritizing what truly matters, resilient individuals can navigate challenges with resilience and clarity, keeping their sights on the bigger picture and ultimately leading a more fulfilling and purposeful life.

Building resilience requires developing a deep sense of self-awareness and understanding. It involves taking the time to explore and identify one's strengths, weaknesses, and values. By understanding oneself on a profound level, individuals can tap into their inner resources and harness their strengths to navigate challenges. They become aware of their limitations and areas for growth, allowing them to seek support and develop new skills. Additionally, knowing their core values provides a guiding compass, helping them make decisions aligned with their authentic selves. This self-awareness empowers individuals to cultivate resilience by leveraging their unique qualities, addressing areas of improvement, and aligning their actions with their values. Through this process, they not only build resilience but also enhance their overall well-being and live a more purposeful and fulfilling life.

15. Mindfulness and Self-Care: Nurturing Our Mental and Emotional Health

In today's fast-paced society, prioritizing mental and emotional health has become increasingly crucial. The constant demands, pressures, and distractions of modern life can easily lead to stress, anxiety, and burnout. Taking the time to prioritize our mental and emotional well-being is essential for maintaining balance, resilience, and overall satisfaction in life. It allows us to better cope with challenges, navigate relationships, and make informed decisions. By recognizing the importance of our mental and emotional health, we can establish healthy boundaries, practice self-care, and seek support when needed. Prioritizing our well-being not only benefits us individually but also positively impacts our relationships, work performance, and overall quality of life. It is a proactive step towards living a more fulfilling and meaningful existence in an increasingly demanding world.

Mindfulness and self-care have proven to be powerful tools in reducing stress and promoting overall well-being. By cultivating a state of present moment awareness, mindfulness allows us to become more attuned to our thoughts, emotions, and bodily sensations without judgment. This practice helps us break free from the grip of stress-inducing thoughts and patterns, allowing for greater clarity and calmness. Self-care, on the other hand, involves engaging in activities that nurture and replenish our physical, mental, and emotional health. This can include practices such as exercise, meditation, spending time in nature, pursuing hobbies, and establishing healthy boundaries. By making time for self-care, we provide ourselves with the necessary space to recharge, rejuvenate, and cultivate a sense of balance. Together, mindfulness and self-care create a powerful synergy, enabling us to navigate the challenges of life with greater resilience, improve our overall well-being, and foster a deeper connection with ourselves and others.

Self-awareness plays a crucial role in practicing effective self-care. It involves tuning into our thoughts, emotions, and physical sensations, and gaining a deep understanding of our own needs, desires, and limits. By developing self-awareness, we become attuned to the signals our body and mind send us, allowing us to recognize when we're feeling overwhelmed, stressed, or depleted. This awareness empowers us to make intentional choices that prioritize our well-being. It helps us identify activities, practices, and habits that nourish and rejuvenate us on a deep level. Self-awareness also helps us recognize when we may be engaging in self-sabotaging behaviors or neglecting our own needs, and encourages us to make adjustments to ensure we're practicing self-care in a way that truly supports our holistic health. By cultivating self-awareness, we can tailor our self-care practices to align with our unique needs and values, leading to a more fulfilling and sustainable approach to nurturing ourselves.

The rapid advancement of technology and the widespread use of social media have undoubtedly transformed the way we connect, communicate, and access information. However, along with its numerous benefits, technology and social media can also have a profound impact on our mental health. The constant exposure to curated and often idealized versions of others' lives, the pressure to constantly be online and available, and the addictive nature of scrolling and seeking validation can contribute to feelings of anxiety, comparison, and diminished self-esteem. In this digital age, intentional self-care practices are more important than ever. Taking breaks from technology, setting boundaries around screen time, and engaging in activities that promote mindfulness and presence can help restore balance and protect our mental well-being. Cultivating meaningful connections, engaging in hobbies, and spending time in nature are essential components of intentional self-care that can counteract the negative effects of technology and social media. By consciously nurturing our mental health, we can navigate the digital landscape in a healthier and more balanced way, ensuring that technology enhances our lives rather than detracts from our well-being.

Incorporating mindfulness into daily routines can have a profound impact on our well-being and overall mental health. One effective strategy is to set aside dedicated time for meditation or deep breathing exercises. Taking just a few minutes each day to sit in stillness, focus on the present moment, and observe our thoughts and sensations without judgment can help us cultivate a sense of inner calm and clarity. Engaging in deep breathing exercises, such as diaphragmatic breathing or box breathing, can activate the body's relaxation response and reduce stress levels. Additionally, integrating mindfulness into everyday activities can be beneficial. For example, paying attention to the sensations of eating during meals, fully immersing ourselves in the task at hand, or taking mindful walks in nature can bring us back to the present moment and foster a greater sense of peace and connection. By consistently practicing these mindfulness strategies, we can enhance our self-awareness, manage stress more effectively, and cultivate a greater sense of overall well-being.

Setting boundaries and learning to say "no" are crucial steps in prioritizing self-care and maintaining our overall well-being. In today's fast-paced and demanding world, it's easy to become overwhelmed by the constant demands and expectations placed upon us. However, by establishing clear boundaries and being assertive in communicating our needs, we can protect our time, energy, and emotional well-being. Saying "no" when necessary allows us to focus on what truly matters to us and allocate our resources in a way that aligns with our values and priorities. It empowers us to create space for self-care activities, rest, and rejuvenation. While it may feel uncomfortable initially, setting boundaries not only helps us prevent burnout and reduce stress but also promotes healthier relationships and mutual respect. By honoring our own limits and needs, we send a message to ourselves and others that our well-being is important and deserving of attention. Ultimately, embracing the power of setting boundaries and saying "no" enables us to live more authentically, take better care of ourselves, and cultivate a greater sense of balance and fulfillment in our lives.

Self-care and resilience are closely intertwined when it comes to navigating adversity and overcoming challenges. Engaging in regular self-care practices not only supports our overall well-being but also builds our capacity to bounce back from difficult situations. Taking care of ourselves physically, emotionally, and mentally equips us with the strength and resources needed to face life's ups and downs with greater resilience. By prioritizing self-care, we cultivate a strong foundation of self-nurturance and self-compassion, which empowers us to handle stress, setbacks, and setbacks with greater ease. Whether it's carving out time for relaxation, engaging in activities that bring us joy, seeking support from loved ones, or practicing mindfulness, self-care acts as a crucial pillar in our resilience toolkit. It replenishes our energy, enhances our coping mechanisms, and fosters a positive mindset, allowing us to adapt and thrive in the face of adversity.

Self-compassion plays a vital role in nurturing our mental and emotional health. It involves treating ourselves with kindness, understanding, and acceptance, especially during times of difficulty or self-criticism. Instead of being self-judgmental or harsh, self-compassion encourages us to offer ourselves the same care and compassion we would extend to a loved one. By cultivating self-compassion, we create a nurturing inner environment where we can acknowledge our pain, mistakes, and vulnerabilities without judgment or shame. It allows us to embrace our humanity and recognize that suffering is a universal part of the human experience. Through self-compassion, we develop a supportive and loving relationship with ourselves, fostering resilience, self-esteem, and emotional well-being. It helps us cultivate a greater sense of self-worth, inner strength, and the ability to navigate life's challenges with greater self-acceptance and resilience.

Engaging in hobbies and activities that bring joy and relaxation offers numerous benefits for our mental and emotional well-being. These activities provide a much-needed break from the demands of daily life, allowing us to recharge and rejuvenate. When we immerse ourselves in activities we enjoy, whether it's painting, playing an instrument, gardening, or reading, we enter a state of flow where time seems to slip away and we feel fully present in the moment. This experience of flow can bring a sense of fulfillment and satisfaction. Hobbies also serve as a form of self-expression, allowing us to tap into our creativity and explore our interests. They provide an outlet for stress and negative emotions, offering a healthy and productive way to cope with challenges. Moreover, engaging in activities we love can enhance our overall well-being by promoting a sense of accomplishment, boosting self-esteem, and fostering a positive mindset. It reminds us to prioritize self-care and enjoy the simple pleasures in life, ultimately contributing to a more balanced and fulfilling existence.

Rest and sleep play a vital role in promoting overall well-being. In today's fast-paced and demanding world, it can be easy to overlook the importance of giving our bodies and minds adequate time to rest and recharge. Quality sleep is essential for various aspects of our health, including cognitive function, emotional well-being, immune system function, and physical vitality. During sleep, our bodies undergo essential processes that support cellular repair, memory consolidation, hormone regulation, and overall rejuvenation. Lack of sleep or poor-quality sleep can lead to a range of negative effects, such as increased stress, decreased focus and productivity, impaired decision-making, weakened immune function, and heightened risk of mental health issues. Prioritizing rest and sleep means recognizing their role in maintaining optimal health and performance. By establishing consistent sleep routines, creating a comfortable sleep environment, and practicing relaxation techniques, we can enhance the quality and duration of our sleep, promoting a greater sense of well-being, energy, and vitality in our daily lives. Taking the time to rest and prioritize sleep is not a luxury but an essential component of a healthy and balanced lifestyle.

Nutrition and exercise play a crucial role in supporting mental and emotional health. The food we consume provides the necessary nutrients for brain function and the production of neurotransmitters that regulate our moods and emotions. A balanced diet rich in fruits, vegetables, whole grains, lean proteins, and healthy fats can contribute to improved cognitive function, increased energy levels, and a more stable emotional state. Regular exercise, on the other hand, has been shown to release endorphins, the feel-good hormones that can elevate mood, reduce stress, and improve overall mental well-being. Physical activity also promotes better sleep, boosts self-confidence, and provides a healthy outlet for managing stress and anxiety. Engaging in regular exercise, whether it's through aerobic activities, strength training, or mind-body practices like yoga or tai chi, can have profound effects on our mental and emotional health. By nourishing our bodies with nutritious foods and engaging in regular physical activity, we provide ourselves with a solid foundation for maintaining optimal mental and emotional well-being.

Regular check-ins with oneself are essential to assess and adjust self-care practices. Life is constantly changing, and our needs and priorities fluctuate along with it. Taking the time to pause, reflect, and check in with ourselves allows us to evaluate how our self-care routines are serving us and whether any adjustments are needed. It's a chance to tune into our emotions, physical sensations, and overall well-being. Are we feeling overwhelmed, stressed, or depleted? Are there signs of burnout or neglecting certain aspects of self-care? By engaging in regular self-reflection, we can identify areas that require more attention or improvements, and then make the necessary adjustments to support our overall well-being. This may involve modifying our self-care practices, setting new boundaries, seeking additional support, or simply giving ourselves permission to prioritize our needs. Regular check-ins empower us to be proactive in nurturing our mental, emotional, and physical health, ensuring that our self-care practices remain aligned with our ever-evolving needs.

Negative self-talk can have a profound impact on our mental and emotional well-being. The constant stream of self-critical thoughts and beliefs can chip away at our self-esteem, create a negative self-image, and hinder our personal growth. It is essential to recognize the power of our internal dialogue and actively work towards cultivating a positive self-image. By challenging negative self-talk and replacing it with self-compassion, self-acceptance, and self-affirmation, we can transform our relationship with ourselves. Cultivating a positive self-image involves acknowledging our strengths, celebrating our achievements, and embracing our unique qualities. Through mindful awareness and intentional efforts, we can foster a more loving and supportive inner dialogue, paving the way for greater self-confidence, resilience, and overall well-being.

Seeking support and connecting with others can have profound benefits for our mental and emotional health. Human beings are inherently social creatures, and having a sense of connection and belonging is crucial for our well-being. When we reach out for support, whether it's from friends, family, or professionals, we create a space where our experiences can be understood and validated. Sharing our struggles and challenges with others not only lightens the emotional burden but also opens the door to different perspectives and insights. Engaging in meaningful relationships and fostering a support network can provide a sense of comfort, empathy, and encouragement. It reminds us that we are not alone in our journey and that there are people who care about our well-being. By nurturing these connections and seeking support, we create an environment that fosters healing, resilience, and personal growth.

Therapy and counseling play a vital role in developing effective self-care practices. These professional interventions provide a safe and supportive space for individuals to explore their thoughts, emotions, and behaviors. Therapists and counselors are trained to guide individuals in understanding the underlying causes of their struggles and helping them develop strategies to improve their mental and emotional well-being. Through therapy, individuals can gain insights into their patterns of self-care, identify areas for improvement, and learn new coping skills. Therapists can also provide valuable guidance in setting boundaries, managing stress, and cultivating self-compassion. Additionally, therapy and counseling offer a non-judgmental and confidential environment where individuals can express their concerns and receive objective feedback. By working collaboratively with a therapist or counselor, individuals can develop personalized self-care plans tailored to their unique needs, fostering greater self-awareness, resilience, and overall well-being.

Mindfulness-based interventions have proven to be immensely valuable in reducing symptoms of anxiety and depression. These interventions emphasize the practice of mindfulness, which involves bringing one's attention to the present moment with a non-judgmental and accepting attitude. By cultivating this awareness, individuals can develop a greater understanding of their thoughts, emotions, and bodily sensations. Mindfulness helps individuals recognize the patterns of negative thinking and rumination that often contribute to anxiety and depression. Through regular practice, individuals can learn to observe their thoughts and emotions without becoming entangled in them, gaining a sense of perspective and reducing reactivity. Mindfulness-based interventions also teach individuals practical techniques such as deep breathing exercises and body scans to promote relaxation and reduce physiological symptoms of anxiety and depression. By incorporating mindfulness into their daily lives, individuals can experience a greater sense of calm, increased self-compassion, and improved emotional well-being.

The importance of self-care cannot be overstated for individuals in high-stress professions or caregiving roles. These individuals often dedicate themselves to the well-being and needs of others, which can leave them feeling emotionally and physically drained. Self-care is crucial to prevent burnout and maintain overall well-being. Engaging in regular self-care practices helps these individuals recharge, rejuvenate, and restore their energy levels. It allows them to replenish their mental and emotional resources, enabling them to continue providing care and support to others effectively. Self-care activities may vary depending on individual preferences, but they can include activities such as exercise, mindfulness, hobbies, spending time in nature, seeking social support, or engaging in relaxation techniques. By prioritizing self-care, individuals in high-stress professions or caregiving roles can ensure their own well-being, which ultimately enhances their ability to fulfill their responsibilities and maintain a sustainable work-life balance. It is a proactive and essential step towards preserving their mental, emotional, and physical health.

The connection between self-care and overall life satisfaction is significant and profound. When we prioritize our physical, mental, and emotional well-being through self-care practices, we enhance our overall quality of life. Taking the time to engage in activities that nurture and rejuvenate us allows us to recharge and maintain a healthy balance. It helps us manage stress, improve our resilience, and cultivate a positive mindset. By caring for ourselves, we are better equipped to handle the challenges and demands of daily life. Self-care promotes self-awareness and self-compassion, enabling us to better understand and meet our own needs. When we prioritize self-care, we are sending a powerful message to ourselves that we deserve to be cared for and that our well-being matters. This sense of self-worth and self-nurturing translates into greater life satisfaction, as we experience increased happiness, fulfillment, and a deeper sense of inner peace. Ultimately, self-care is an investment in our own happiness and well-being, and it has the potential to positively impact every aspect of our lives.

The practice of gratitude and mindfulness has transformative effects on mental and emotional health. When we cultivate a sense of gratitude, we shift our focus from what is lacking to what we already have, fostering a mindset of abundance and appreciation. This simple act of recognizing and acknowledging the positive aspects of our lives can significantly improve our overall well-being. By directing our attention to the present moment through mindfulness, we become more aware of our thoughts, emotions, and sensations without judgment. This awareness allows us to observe and accept our experiences with compassion and curiosity, reducing stress and promoting a greater sense of inner peace. Both gratitude and mindfulness empower us to cultivate positive emotions, foster resilience, and enhance our overall mental and emotional health. They provide us with tools to navigate life's challenges, helping us find joy in small moments, nurture meaningful connections, and find solace in times of difficulty. Incorporating gratitude and mindfulness into our daily lives can lead to a profound shift in perspective, allowing us to cultivate a deeper sense of contentment, happiness, and fulfillment.

Incorporating self-care practices into our busy schedules is essential for maintaining our mental and emotional well-being. Despite the demands of daily life, finding moments for self-care is crucial. One effective strategy is to schedule dedicated "me time" in our calendars, treating it as a non-negotiable appointment with ourselves. This can be as simple as setting aside a specific time each day or week to engage in activities that replenish and recharge us. Taking regular breaks throughout the day, even if it's just a few minutes to stretch, breathe deeply, or engage in a quick mindfulness exercise, can also have a significant impact on our well-being. Additionally, delegating tasks, setting boundaries, and learning to say "no" when necessary allows us to protect our time and energy. It's important to remember that self-care doesn't always have to be extravagant or time-consuming. It can be as simple as indulging in a favorite hobby, practicing self-compassion, or prioritizing activities that bring us joy and relaxation. By consciously incorporating self-care strategies into our routines, we can create a sustainable and nourishing self-care practice that supports our overall health and happiness.

Mindfulness, the practice of intentionally paying attention to the present moment without judgment, plays a significant role in reducing stress and enhancing decision-making. By cultivating mindfulness, we become more aware of our thoughts, emotions, and bodily sensations, allowing us to recognize and respond to stressors more effectively. Regular mindfulness practice has been shown to activate the relaxation response and reduce the physiological and psychological symptoms of stress. It helps us develop a greater sense of clarity and focus, enabling us to make better decisions by approaching situations with a calm and balanced mindset. Mindfulness also enhances our ability to regulate our emotions, reducing impulsive reactions and increasing our capacity to respond thoughtfully and rationally. By anchoring ourselves in the present moment, we can better assess the available options, consider the consequences, and make choices aligned with our values and long-term goals. Overall, mindfulness empowers us to navigate life's challenges with greater resilience, equanimity, and wisdom, leading to improved well-being and more informed decision-making.

Self-acceptance and self-love are fundamental pillars in nurturing mental and emotional health. Embracing and fully accepting ourselves, flaws and all, is essential for building a strong foundation of self-worth and resilience. When we practice self-acceptance, we acknowledge our inherent value as human beings and release the need for perfection or comparison. This allows us to cultivate a compassionate and non-judgmental attitude towards ourselves, fostering a sense of inner peace and contentment. Self-love involves treating ourselves with kindness, compassion, and care, just as we would with a dear friend. It means prioritizing our well-being, setting boundaries, and engaging in activities that bring us joy and fulfillment. When we love ourselves, we create a safe and supportive internal environment where we can grow, heal, and thrive. Self-acceptance and self-love empower us to navigate life's challenges with greater resilience and authenticity, forming the basis for healthy relationships, fulfilling pursuits, and overall well-being. By embracing who we are and extending love to ourselves, we unlock the potential for personal growth, meaningful connections, and a profound sense of inner fulfillment.

The connection between physical self-care and mental and emotional well-being is undeniable. Our physical well-being directly influences our mental and emotional state, and vice versa. Engaging in regular exercise, eating a balanced and nutritious diet, and prioritizing adequate sleep are all essential components of physical self-care. Exercise releases endorphins, which are natural mood elevators, and helps reduce stress and anxiety. Nourishing our bodies with healthy food provides the nutrients necessary for optimal brain function and emotional stability. Sufficient sleep allows our minds and bodies to rest, recharge, and process emotions effectively. When we prioritize physical self-care, we increase our resilience to stress, enhance our overall mood, and improve our ability to cope with life's challenges. Taking care of our physical health not only improves our energy levels and physical vitality but also contributes to greater self-confidence and a positive self-image. By recognizing and honoring the connection between physical and mental well-being, we create a solid foundation for holistic self-care, allowing us to lead balanced, fulfilling, and emotionally healthy lives.

The impact of cultural attitudes and societal expectations on self-care practices cannot be underestimated. Cultural norms and societal pressures often dictate how individuals prioritize their time, energy, and well-being. In some cultures, there may be a strong emphasis on productivity, achievement, and putting others' needs before one's own, which can lead to neglecting self-care. Additionally, societal expectations may reinforce the idea that self-care is selfish or indulgent, discouraging individuals from engaging in activities that promote their well-being. These attitudes can create barriers to practicing self-care and contribute to feelings of guilt, shame, or burnout. However, it is crucial to recognize that self-care is not a luxury but a necessity for maintaining mental, emotional, and physical health. Challenging cultural attitudes and societal expectations surrounding self-care is essential for individuals to prioritize their well-being without guilt or judgment. By promoting a culture of self-care and redefining it as an act of self-preservation rather than selfishness, we can empower individuals to make their well-being a priority and foster healthier, more balanced lives.

The need for ongoing self-reflection and adaptation in developing effective self-care practices is essential for maintaining balance and well-being. Self-care is not a one-size-fits-all approach, as our needs and circumstances change over time. Engaging in regular self-reflection allows us to assess our current state of well-being and identify areas that require attention and care. By examining our physical, mental, and emotional needs, we can make informed decisions about the self-care practices that will best support us. Furthermore, adapting our self-care practices as needed allows us to respond to the evolving demands and challenges of our lives. It requires a willingness to experiment, try new strategies, and let go of what no longer serves us. Ongoing self-reflection and adaptation foster a dynamic and personalized self-care routine that aligns with our individual needs, preferences, and goals. By continuously evaluating and adjusting our self-care practices, we can cultivate a resilient foundation of well-being that supports us in navigating the complexities of life with greater balance and vitality.

16. From Victim to Survivor: Turning Trauma into Empowerment

Recognizing the difference between victimhood and survival is a powerful mindset shift that empowers individuals to take control of their lives. Victimhood perpetuates a sense of powerlessness and resignation, where one feels at the mercy of external circumstances and blames others for their misfortunes. On the other hand, adopting a survival mindset acknowledges the challenges and adversities one has faced but refuses to be defined by them. It involves taking ownership of one's experiences and choices, and actively seeking ways to overcome obstacles and thrive. Shifting from victimhood to survival requires a change in perspective, allowing oneself to see the strength, resilience, and resourcefulness within. It involves reframing setbacks as opportunities for growth and learning, and embracing personal agency to create positive change. By embracing a survival mindset, individuals can tap into their inner strength, reclaim their power, and move forward with a renewed sense of purpose and empowerment.

Acknowledging the impact of trauma on mental health is a crucial step towards healing and recovery. Traumatic experiences can deeply affect individuals, causing emotional distress, anxiety, depression, and other mental health challenges. It is essential to recognize that trauma is not a sign of weakness but a valid response to overwhelming circumstances. Seeking appropriate professional support, such as therapy or counseling, can provide a safe and supportive space to process and heal from trauma. Mental health professionals trained in trauma-informed care can offer specialized interventions and evidence-based approaches to address the unique needs and challenges associated with trauma. Through therapy, individuals can gain insight, develop coping strategies, and gradually restore a sense of safety, trust, and well-being. It is important to remember that healing from trauma is a journey, and seeking professional support is a proactive and empowering step towards reclaiming one's life and fostering resilience.

Understanding that the path to empowerment may involve facing difficult emotions and memories is an important aspect of personal growth and healing. While it can be challenging and uncomfortable to confront painful experiences, it is through this process that individuals can gain a deeper understanding of themselves and their resilience. By acknowledging and allowing space for these emotions and memories, individuals can gradually release their hold and reclaim a sense of control over their lives. This journey often requires courage, self-compassion, and the support of trusted individuals or professionals. By facing these difficult aspects head-on, individuals can begin to untangle the web of pain and disempowerment, paving the way for growth, healing, and a renewed sense of empowerment. It is important to approach this process at a pace that feels manageable, ensuring self-care and support are prioritized along the way. With time and patience, facing difficult emotions and memories can lead to a profound transformation, allowing individuals to reclaim their personal power and create a more empowered and fulfilling life.

Identifying and challenging limiting beliefs that may stem from past traumas is a crucial step towards empowerment and personal growth. Traumatic experiences can shape our perceptions of ourselves and the world, leading to negative and self-limiting beliefs that hinder our progress and well-being. By becoming aware of these beliefs and their origins, we can begin to question their validity and challenge their hold on us. It requires a willingness to explore the deeper layers of our thoughts and emotions, and a commitment to self-reflection and self-compassion. Through therapy, counseling, or self-guided introspection, we can examine the narratives we have internalized and replace them with more empowering and supportive beliefs. This process involves recognizing that these limiting beliefs were formed as adaptive responses to trauma, but they no longer serve us in our present lives. By actively challenging and reframing these beliefs, we can break free from their constraints and create new narratives that align with our true potential. It is an ongoing journey that requires patience and persistence, but the rewards are immense. By dismantling limiting beliefs, we open ourselves up to new possibilities, greater self-confidence, and a renewed sense of agency in shaping our lives.

Developing coping strategies to manage triggers and promote emotional regulation is an essential aspect of personal growth and resilience. Triggers are events, situations, or even internal thoughts and memories that activate intense emotional reactions linked to past traumas or distressing experiences. Recognizing our triggers and understanding how they affect us is the first step in building effective coping mechanisms. This may involve seeking professional help, such as therapy or counseling, to gain insight into our triggers and learn strategies for managing them. Coping strategies can vary from person to person but often include techniques like deep breathing exercises, grounding techniques, mindfulness practices, and self-soothing activities. These strategies help us regulate our emotions, reduce anxiety and stress, and regain a sense of control when triggered. It's important to remember that coping strategies take time to develop and refine, and it's okay to seek support along the way. By actively working on managing triggers and promoting emotional regulation, we empower ourselves to navigate challenging situations with greater resilience, maintain healthier relationships, and enhance our overall well-being.

Finding community and support networks of other survivors can be a powerful source of validation and connection on the journey to healing and empowerment. Connecting with individuals who have experienced similar traumas or challenges can provide a sense of understanding and empathy that is difficult to find elsewhere. These communities create a safe space where survivors can openly share their stories, emotions, and experiences without fear of judgment or invalidation. By connecting with others who have walked a similar path, survivors can gain validation for their feelings and experiences, realizing they are not alone in their struggles. These support networks offer a platform for sharing coping strategies, offering mutual support, and learning from one another's resilience. Together, survivors can celebrate milestones, share successes, and offer each other strength during difficult times. Building these connections not only promotes healing and personal growth but also fosters a sense of belonging and empowerment. Through community and support networks, survivors can find solace, encouragement, and the reassurance that they are not defined by their past but are part of a resilient collective that is working towards healing and reclaiming their lives.

Reframing the narrative of past traumas from one of victimhood to one of growth and resilience is a transformative process that empowers individuals to reclaim their stories and reshape their identities. It involves challenging the belief that being a victim defines their entire existence and shifting the focus towards the strength and resilience that emerged from those experiences. By acknowledging the challenges they have faced and the lessons learned, survivors can begin to see themselves as resilient individuals who have not only endured but also grown stronger through adversity. Reframing the narrative allows individuals to reinterpret their experiences, emphasizing personal growth, self-discovery, and empowerment. It involves recognizing that they have the power to redefine their own story, to break free from the limitations imposed by the past, and to create a future based on their strengths and aspirations. This process is not about denying or minimizing the pain of past traumas but rather about embracing the opportunity for personal transformation and cultivating a sense of agency and empowerment. By reframing their narrative, individuals can rewrite their own story, emphasizing resilience, growth, and their ability to thrive in the face of adversity.

Practicing self-compassion and self-care is a vital component of healing and restoring one's sense of self-worth after experiencing trauma or challenging life circumstances. It involves treating oneself with kindness, understanding, and patience, recognizing that self-compassion is not selfish but rather a necessary act of self-preservation. By nurturing oneself through self-care practices such as engaging in activities that bring joy, setting boundaries, and prioritizing rest and relaxation, individuals can replenish their emotional reserves and create a safe space for healing. Self-compassion involves embracing imperfections and accepting oneself unconditionally, acknowledging that everyone experiences pain and struggles. It requires challenging self-critical thoughts and replacing them with self-affirming and supportive beliefs. By practicing self-compassion and self-care, individuals honor their own worth and validate their experiences, paving the way for healing, resilience, and the restoration of a strong sense of self-worth.

Fostering a sense of meaning and purpose beyond the trauma is a powerful way to reclaim one's identity and move forward in the healing journey. Engaging in activities that bring joy and fulfillment can provide a much-needed respite from the pain and challenges of the past. It involves reconnecting with personal passions, interests, and values, and actively pursuing activities that align with them. By immersing oneself in activities that evoke a sense of purpose and fulfillment, individuals can tap into their inherent strengths and talents, rediscover their passions, and rebuild a sense of identity that extends beyond the trauma. These activities may vary from creative pursuits, volunteering, advocating for causes, or cultivating meaningful relationships. By actively seeking out moments of joy and fulfillment, individuals create new narratives that expand beyond the traumatic experiences, reminding themselves of their capacity for growth, resilience, and the ability to find meaning and purpose in life once again.

Mindfulness practices offer a powerful tool for grounding oneself in the present moment and cultivating self-awareness. By intentionally focusing our attention on the present, we can become more attuned to our thoughts, emotions, and bodily sensations. Through practices like meditation, deep breathing exercises, or body scans, we can develop a greater understanding of our inner experiences. Mindfulness allows us to observe our thoughts and feelings without judgment, creating space for self-reflection and insight. This heightened self-awareness enables us to better navigate challenges, make conscious choices, and respond to life's ups and downs with greater clarity and equanimity. By incorporating mindfulness into our daily lives, we can cultivate a deeper connection to ourselves and the world around us, enhancing our overall well-being and fostering a greater sense of inner peace.

Examining and shifting negative self-talk and self-blame that may have resulted from past trauma is a crucial step in the healing process. Traumatic experiences can often lead to internalizing harmful beliefs about oneself, such as feeling unworthy, responsible for the trauma, or fundamentally flawed. Recognizing and challenging these negative narratives is essential for reclaiming one's self-worth and building a positive self-image. It involves developing self-compassion and practicing self-acceptance, understanding that the trauma was not your fault and that you are deserving of love and healing. By reframing negative self-talk and replacing it with affirming and empowering thoughts, you can cultivate a healthier and more compassionate relationship with yourself. This process may involve seeking professional support, engaging in therapeutic techniques such as cognitive-behavioral therapy (CBT), and surrounding yourself with a supportive network that validates your experiences and helps you reframe your perspective. Over time, you can transform the way you talk to yourself, fostering self-love, resilience, and a stronger sense of self.

Utilizing creative outlets such as writing, art, or music can be a powerful means of expression and processing of emotions. When dealing with the aftermath of trauma, it can be challenging to articulate and make sense of complex feelings and experiences. Engaging in creative activities provides a safe and non-judgmental space to explore and externalize these emotions. Writing allows for introspection and self-reflection, enabling you to put words to your thoughts and feelings. Art and music provide alternative channels for expression, tapping into the depths of your emotions and allowing for a release that goes beyond words. The act of creating can be cathartic, helping to release pent-up energy and emotions while also providing a sense of control and agency over your narrative. It can be a transformative process of self-discovery, allowing you to reconnect with your inner self and find solace, healing, and empowerment. Whether through writing, painting, playing an instrument, or engaging in any other creative pursuit, these outlets can become powerful tools for self-expression, processing trauma, and reclaiming your voice.

Recognizing the impact of past traumas on relationships is an important step towards healing and growth. Traumatic experiences can leave lasting imprints on our ability to trust, form intimate connections, and navigate conflicts. By acknowledging the ways in which past traumas may have affected our relationships, we can begin to address and heal those wounds. It involves cultivating self-awareness and understanding how trauma may have shaped our perceptions, behaviors, and emotional responses within relationships. Building healthy and supportive connections requires open communication, empathy, and a willingness to address and work through past hurts. It may involve seeking professional help, such as therapy, to gain insight into the impact of trauma on relationship patterns and develop strategies for healthier dynamics. Through this process, we can learn to set boundaries, communicate effectively, and foster trust and intimacy. It takes time, patience, and a commitment to personal growth, but by actively working on our relationships and addressing the effects of trauma, we can create spaces of safety, understanding, and resilience where healing and healthy connections can thrive.

Embracing vulnerability is a powerful way to cultivate authentic and meaningful connections with others. While it may feel uncomfortable or risky, allowing ourselves to be vulnerable opens the door to genuine intimacy and emotional growth. When we share our fears, insecurities, and struggles with trusted individuals, we create a space for empathy, understanding, and support. Vulnerability invites others to reciprocate and share their own experiences, fostering a deeper sense of connection and shared humanity. It requires us to let go of the armor we may have built to protect ourselves and instead lean into our authentic selves. By embracing vulnerability, we acknowledge that it is okay to be imperfect, to have needs, and to seek comfort and validation from others. This practice not only enhances our relationships but also promotes personal growth as we confront and work through our own emotional barriers. It allows us to develop resilience, expand our emotional range, and experience the transformative power of vulnerability in creating genuine connections that enrich our lives.

Learning to set healthy boundaries is a vital step in protecting oneself from re-traumatization. It involves recognizing and honoring one's own needs, limits, and values, and communicating them assertively and respectfully to others. By establishing clear boundaries, individuals create a safe and secure space for themselves, where they can maintain their physical, emotional, and psychological well-being. This may involve setting limits on the behaviors and actions of others, as well as taking responsibility for self-care and prioritizing one's own needs. Boundaries act as a protective shield, preventing the intrusion of harmful or triggering experiences that can reawaken past traumas. They allow individuals to create a sense of safety and control in their lives, fostering a healing environment where they can rebuild trust, establish healthy relationships, and nurture their own growth and recovery. Learning to set and enforce boundaries is a powerful act of self-empowerment, allowing individuals to regain a sense of agency and create a space where their trauma does not define them or dictate their future.

Understanding that the journey from victim to survivor is not linear is crucial in the healing process. It is common to experience setbacks and relapses along the way, as healing is a complex and individualized process. There may be moments when past traumas resurface, triggering intense emotions and challenging the progress made. It's important to approach these setbacks with self-compassion and patience, recognizing that they are a natural part of the healing journey. Acknowledging and validating these experiences can help individuals navigate through them with resilience and determination. It is normal to have ups and downs, and setbacks should not be seen as failures, but rather as opportunities for further growth and self-reflection. Each setback can serve as a reminder of the strength and resilience that has already been cultivated. By embracing the non-linear nature of healing, individuals can find solace in the understanding that setbacks do not define their progress, but rather contribute to their overall resilience and ability to thrive in the face of adversity.

Practicing forgiveness towards oneself and others involved in past traumas can be a powerful tool for promoting emotional healing. Holding onto anger, resentment, or blame can keep us trapped in a cycle of pain and prevent us from moving forward. Forgiveness doesn't mean condoning or forgetting the harm that was done, but rather it is a choice to release ourselves from the grip of bitterness and reclaim our own emotional well-being. It involves acknowledging the pain, accepting the past, and consciously choosing to let go of negative emotions. Forgiveness allows us to free ourselves from the burden of carrying the weight of past traumas, enabling us to heal and create space for personal growth. It's important to remember that forgiveness is a process, and it may take time and effort. It involves compassionately understanding our own wounds and the wounds of others, and finding a place of empathy and peace within ourselves. By practicing forgiveness, we can reclaim our power, cultivate inner peace, and open ourselves up to new possibilities of healing and growth.

Finding meaning in the struggle and using past traumas as a means of helping others or advocating for change can be a transformative and empowering process. When we have experienced deep pain and adversity, we have the potential to develop a unique perspective and empathy that can inspire and support others who are going through similar challenges. By sharing our stories, speaking out about injustices, or lending a helping hand to those in need, we can turn our past traumas into catalysts for positive change. It is through these acts of service and advocacy that we not only heal ourselves but also create a ripple effect of healing and empowerment in the lives of others. Finding meaning in our own struggles allows us to transcend victimhood and transform our pain into purpose. It is a powerful way to reclaim our agency, reclaim our voice, and make a difference in the world. As we help others navigate their own journeys, we continue to grow and find a renewed sense of meaning and fulfillment in our lives.

Recognizing that the experience of trauma is unique and that everyone's journey towards empowerment will look different is crucial for fostering understanding and compassion. Trauma affects individuals in diverse ways, and there is no one-size-fits-all approach to healing and empowerment. Each person's story, resilience, and resources are unique, and it is important to honor and respect the individuality of their experiences. This understanding helps to create a safe and inclusive space where survivors can share their stories, express their emotions, and support one another without judgment. By acknowledging and validating the uniqueness of each person's journey, we create an environment that promotes healing, growth, and empowerment. We embrace the diverse paths individuals take towards finding their inner strength and reclaiming their lives, understanding that their experiences and choices are deeply personal and significant. Ultimately, by recognizing and respecting these differences, we foster a culture of empathy, acceptance, and empowerment for all survivors.

Celebrating small victories and progress towards healing is an essential aspect of the journey towards empowerment and resilience. Healing from trauma is a complex and ongoing process that requires courage, strength, and perseverance. Along this path, it is crucial to acknowledge and celebrate the small steps forward, as they represent significant achievements and milestones in one's healing journey. By recognizing and honoring these victories, survivors can gain a sense of validation, self-worth, and motivation to continue their progress. Celebrating these moments also serves as a reminder of the resilience and strength that resides within, fueling the belief that healing is possible. It reinforces the idea that every small step counts and that even in the face of adversity, progress can be made. By celebrating these victories, survivors cultivate a positive and empowering mindset, fostering self-motivation, and building resilience. It becomes a testament to their resilience and a source of inspiration for others who may be on a similar path.

17. The Power of Forgiveness: Letting Go of Resentment and Moving Forward

Forgiveness is indeed a powerful tool for releasing feelings of resentment and anger towards those who have caused us harm. When we hold onto anger and resentment, it can weigh us down and negatively impact our well-being. By choosing to forgive, we free ourselves from the burden of carrying those negative emotions. Forgiveness does not mean forgetting or condoning the actions of others, but rather, it is a conscious decision to let go of the pain and release ourselves from the grip of the past. It is a process that requires self-reflection, empathy, and understanding. By choosing forgiveness, we reclaim our power and take control of our own emotional well-being. It allows us to heal and move forward with our lives, fostering inner peace, and creating space for personal growth and transformation. Moreover, forgiveness can be a profound act of self-love and self-care, as it promotes healing and restores our emotional balance. By practicing forgiveness, we empower ourselves to break free from the chains of resentment and anger, allowing us to cultivate healthier relationships and live more fulfilling lives.

Letting go of resentments can indeed lead to greater emotional and mental well-being. When we hold onto resentments, we carry a heavy emotional burden that can weigh us down and affect various aspects of our lives. Resentment can consume our thoughts, fuel negative emotions, and strain our relationships. By choosing to let go of resentments, we free ourselves from this emotional baggage and create space for healing and growth. It allows us to release the negative energy that keeps us stuck in the past and prevents us from fully embracing the present. Letting go of resentments does not mean forgetting or condoning the past, but rather, it involves accepting what has happened and choosing to move forward with forgiveness and compassion. It is a process that requires self-reflection, self-care, and sometimes seeking support from others. By releasing resentments, we open ourselves up to greater peace, happiness, and overall well-being. We can cultivate healthier relationships, experience increased emotional freedom, and create a more positive and fulfilling life for ourselves.

Forgiveness indeed involves accepting what has happened and finding a way to move forward. It is a deeply personal and transformative process that allows us to release the grip of anger, hurt, and resentment that may have been holding us back. Forgiveness does not mean condoning or forgetting the actions that caused us pain, nor does it require reconciliation or minimizing the impact of the hurtful behavior. Instead, it is a conscious choice to let go of the emotional burden and free ourselves from the negative effects of holding onto grudges. It involves acknowledging our own pain and choosing to release the attachment to the past, allowing ourselves to heal and create space for growth and healing. By practicing forgiveness, we can reclaim our power, restore our inner peace, and create a more positive and compassionate outlook on life. It is a courageous act of self-care and liberation that can bring profound healing and restoration to our mental, emotional, and even physical well-being.

Absolutely, forgiveness is not about condoning or excusing harmful behavior. It's a deeply personal and empowering choice that we make for ourselves. When we hold onto resentment, anger, or grudges, it only perpetuates our own suffering and keeps us trapped in a cycle of negativity. By choosing forgiveness, we are not absolving the person or their actions, but rather releasing the emotional burden and reclaiming our own emotional freedom. It's an act of self-compassion and self-care, recognizing that we deserve to let go of the pain and live our lives without being constantly weighed down by the past. Forgiveness allows us to break free from the chains of bitterness and resentment, and it empowers us to move forward with greater peace, happiness, and personal growth. It's a courageous and transformative choice that can lead to a sense of liberation and emotional well-being.

Forgiveness is a transformative act of liberation that frees us from the shackles of resentment and anger. It is not an easy journey, but a courageous and empowering one. Forgiveness does not mean forgetting or condoning the hurtful actions of others; rather, it is a personal choice to release the burden of carrying emotional baggage. It is a conscious decision to let go of the pain, reclaim our power, and create space for healing and growth. By embracing forgiveness, we allow ourselves to break free from the cycle of negativity and open our hearts to compassion and understanding. It is a profound act of self-love and self-care, offering us the opportunity to cultivate inner peace and reclaim our emotional well-being.

Forgiveness requires a willingness to let go of negative emotions and to focus on healing and growth. It is not an easy process, but it is a transformative one. By choosing to forgive, we release ourselves from the burden of carrying resentment and anger. It does not mean that we condone or excuse the harmful actions of others, but rather, it allows us to reclaim our power and reclaim control over our own emotional well-being. Forgiveness is a journey of self-discovery, a process of accepting what has happened and finding a way to move forward. It is a way of freeing ourselves from the past and creating space for healing, inner peace, and personal growth.

Forgiveness is a profound and transformative journey that can be both challenging and ongoing. It requires us to confront the pain and hurt that others have caused us, and to navigate our own complex emotions and experiences. Yet, as difficult as it may be, forgiveness has the power to liberate and empower us. It frees us from the shackles of resentment and bitterness, allowing us to reclaim our own inner peace and emotional well-being. By choosing forgiveness, we release ourselves from the burden of carrying grudges and anger, opening the door to healing, growth, and a renewed sense of freedom.

Forgiveness is not about erasing or disregarding the past; it is about finding a way to integrate it into our lives in a healthy and transformative manner. It does not mean that we forget the pain or deny the impact of the past events. Instead, forgiveness invites us to acknowledge and honor our experiences while choosing to let go of the heavy burden they carry. It is a process of embracing the truth of what has happened and finding a path towards healing and growth. By forgiving, we reclaim our power and regain control over our own narrative.

When we are able to forgive, we let go of the anger, resentment, and pain that we have been carrying. This can create space for empathy, compassion, and understanding towards others. Through forgiveness, we may come to realize that those who have hurt us may have also been carrying their own burdens, and may have acted out of their own unresolved pain. By extending forgiveness, we can break the cycle of hurt and resentment and open ourselves up to deeper connections with others. Ultimately, forgiveness can be a powerful tool for fostering greater compassion and understanding in our relationships and communities.

Forgiveness has the power to break destructive cycles of anger and resentment that can persist within families and communities. When we hold onto grudges and refuse to forgive, we contribute to a cycle of hurt and bitterness that can span generations. However, when we choose to forgive, we disrupt this cycle and create an opportunity for healing and reconciliation. By releasing the burden of anger and resentment, we pave the way for healthier relationships, improved communication, and the possibility of positive change. Forgiveness becomes an act of liberation, not only for ourselves but for the collective wellbeing of our families and communities. It opens the door to healing, growth, and the creation of more harmonious and compassionate relationships that can positively impact future generations.

Forgiveness can be a form of self-care that helps us let go of emotional baggage and move forward in our lives. When we hold on to anger, resentment, or other negative emotions towards someone, it can take a toll on our mental and physical well-being. Forgiving someone who has wronged us can help us release those negative emotions and free up mental and emotional space to focus on our own growth and healing. By practicing forgiveness, we can also cultivate a sense of inner peace and self-compassion, which can have positive ripple effects in our relationships and interactions with others.

Forgiveness is a personal and empowering journey that requires taking responsibility for our own healing and growth, rather than relying on others to change or make amends. It involves acknowledging our own emotions and reactions, and choosing to let go of the negative feelings that may be holding us back. While it may be tempting to wait for an apology or for someone else to take the first step, forgiveness is ultimately a choice we make for ourselves. By taking ownership of our own healing and growth, we are able to break free from the cycle of hurt and resentment, and move towards a more peaceful and fulfilling life.

Forgiveness does not mean allowing harmful behavior to continue. It is important to recognize that setting healthy boundaries is an integral part of the forgiveness process. This involves communicating clearly with the person who has caused harm and taking steps to protect oneself from further harm. It may also involve ending or limiting contact with that person if necessary. By setting boundaries, individuals can prioritize their own safety and well-being while still working towards forgiveness and healing.

Forgiveness is a complex and multifaceted journey that extends beyond a single moment or action. It is not a linear process with a fixed endpoint but rather a dynamic and ongoing exploration of healing and growth. It requires patience, self-compassion, and a willingness to confront and navigate difficult emotions. Each person's experience of forgiveness is unique, influenced by their personal history, values, and the nature of the offense. It may involve periods of reflection, introspection, and introspection, as well as seeking support from trusted individuals or professionals. Forgiveness often requires confronting pain, anger, and grief, and acknowledging the impact of the offense. It is a process that can be cyclical, with moments of progress and setbacks, as old wounds resurface or new insights emerge. Through self-reflection, self-compassion, and a commitment to growth, individuals can gradually release the weight of resentment and open themselves to the possibility of healing. It is a courageous act of self-liberation, allowing individuals to reclaim their power, find peace within themselves, and build a brighter future.

Forgiveness is a deeply personal and transformative process that can be supported by seeking assistance from trusted individuals or professionals. Opening up to trusted friends or family members who can provide empathy, understanding, and a non-judgmental space can be invaluable. Sharing our thoughts, feelings, and experiences with others who are supportive and compassionate can help us gain perspective and feel validated. Additionally, seeking the guidance of mental health professionals, such as therapists or counselors, can provide a structured and safe environment to navigate the complexities of forgiveness. These professionals can offer specialized expertise, practical tools, and therapeutic techniques to facilitate healing and growth. Their objective perspective can help us explore the underlying emotions, beliefs, and patterns that may be hindering the forgiveness process. Through their support, we can gain insights, develop coping strategies, and gradually find our way to a place of greater understanding and peace. Remember, seeking support is a sign of strength, and it can provide the necessary resources and guidance to navigate the challenging path towards forgiveness.

Forgiveness is a deeply personal and individual choice that cannot be forced upon or demanded from someone. It is a journey that each person must undertake in their own time and on their own terms. Forcing or pressuring someone to forgive can undermine the healing process and invalidate their emotions and experiences. True forgiveness emerges from a place of genuine understanding, acceptance, and willingness to let go of resentment. It is a decision that arises from within, guided by one's own values, healing needs, and personal growth. Respect for individual autonomy and allowing space for emotions and healing to unfold are essential components in the forgiveness journey. Each person's path towards forgiveness is unique, and it is important to honor and support their right to navigate that journey at their own pace.

Forgiveness has the remarkable ability to shift our focus from the past to the present, allowing us to free ourselves from the shackles of resentment and pain. By choosing forgiveness, we release the grip of past hurts and open ourselves up to the possibilities of the present moment. As we let go of grudges and grievances, we create space within our hearts and minds to embrace the here and now. Forgiveness empowers us to redirect our energy towards cultivating meaning and purpose in our lives. It liberates us from being defined by our past, enabling us to fully engage with the present and embrace opportunities for growth and fulfillment. Through forgiveness, we can embark on a transformative journey of self-discovery, finding new avenues for joy, connection, and personal evolution. It is through this shift in focus that we uncover the beauty and potential that lie in the present, paving the way for a future filled with meaning and purpose.

Forgiveness can be a powerful tool in building stronger and more positive relationships with others. When we hold onto grudges and resentments, it can create a barrier between ourselves and the people around us, preventing us from fully connecting with them. By practicing forgiveness, we open ourselves up to the possibility of deeper and more meaningful relationships. When we let go of the past and focus on the present, we create space for empathy, compassion, and understanding. This can lead to greater intimacy and trust in our relationships, as well as a sense of mutual respect and support. By cultivating forgiveness in our lives, we can create a more positive and fulfilling social network that brings us joy and happiness.

Forgiveness is not always easy, especially when we have been deeply hurt or wronged by someone. However, one approach to forgiveness involves practicing empathy and trying to see things from the perspective of those who have caused us harm. This does not mean excusing or justifying their actions, but rather seeking to understand the factors that may have influenced their behavior. By putting ourselves in their shoes, we can gain insight into their motivations, struggles, and vulnerabilities. This practice of empathy allows us to humanize the person who hurt us, recognizing their flaws and limitations. It helps us recognize that they too may have experienced pain or trauma that influenced their actions. By cultivating empathy, we can develop a broader perspective and begin to let go of anger and resentment, paving the way for forgiveness and healing.

18. Finding Purpose: Identifying Our Passions and Creating Meaningful Lives

Finding our purpose in life is a journey that requires a deep understanding of ourselves and our place in the world. It involves exploring our values, beliefs, and passions to identify what truly matters to us. This process may involve introspection, self-reflection, and experimentation to determine what brings us fulfillment and a sense of purpose. Often, our purpose may be connected to our unique talents and strengths, as well as our life experiences and the challenges we have overcome. By discovering and living our purpose, we can cultivate a greater sense of meaning and fulfillment in our lives, and contribute to the world in a positive way.

Defining our passions can be a powerful tool for discovering our purpose in life. Our passions are often activities or causes that we feel deeply connected to and that bring us joy and a sense of fulfillment. By identifying our passions, we can align our actions with our purpose and begin to create a life that feels meaningful and fulfilling. This can involve exploring different hobbies, volunteering for causes we care about, or simply taking time to reflect on what brings us the most joy and satisfaction. When we are able to connect with our passions and use them as a guide for our actions, we may find ourselves feeling more motivated, energized, and fulfilled in our daily lives.

Finding purpose in life can involve identifying the impact we want to make in the world and working towards achieving that goal. This can include volunteering, engaging in activism, or pursuing a career that aligns with our values and allows us to make a positive difference in the lives of others. When we have a clear understanding of the impact we want to make, it can provide direction and motivation for our actions, and help us prioritize what is truly important to us. By pursuing our purpose in life, we can create a sense of meaning and fulfillment that can improve our overall well-being and contribute to a better world for all.

Engaging in activities that give us a sense of purpose can have a profound impact on our motivation and overall fulfillment in life. When we align our actions with a greater purpose, whether it's through our work, hobbies, or volunteering, we tap into a deeper sense of meaning and connection to something beyond ourselves. These activities provide a sense of direction and a reason to wake up each day with enthusiasm. They ignite our passion, fuel our determination, and inspire us to overcome challenges and setbacks. Having a clear sense of purpose not only enhances our personal satisfaction but also allows us to contribute positively to the world around us. It gives us a sense of fulfillment that goes beyond momentary pleasure and creates a lasting impact on our well-being.

Reflecting on our life experiences is a powerful tool for discovering our strengths, passions, and ultimately, our purpose. Through introspection and thoughtful examination of the challenges we've faced, the lessons we've learned, and the moments that have brought us joy and fulfillment, we can uncover patterns and themes that reveal our true passions. By identifying the activities, skills, and values that resonate deeply with us, we can begin to shape a purpose-driven life. It is through this self-discovery process that we gain a clearer understanding of who we are and what truly matters to us. Armed with this self-awareness, we can make intentional choices that align with our passions and leverage our strengths. By living in alignment with our purpose, we experience a greater sense of fulfillment, meaning, and joy in all aspects of our lives. We become more engaged, energized, and motivated to pursue our dreams and make a positive impact on the world around us.

Embracing our unique qualities and strengths is an essential step in discovering our purpose in life. Each of us possesses a distinct combination of talents, skills, and perspectives that make us who we are. By acknowledging and celebrating these inherent qualities, we can uncover our authentic selves and find clarity in our purpose. Our strengths provide us with the tools to make a meaningful impact on the world. When we embrace these strengths, we gain confidence and resilience, enabling us to navigate challenges and pursue our passions with determination. Our unique qualities allow us to contribute in ways that others cannot, bringing fresh perspectives and innovative solutions to the table. Embracing our uniqueness empowers us to step into our true potential, serving as a guiding light on our journey towards purpose. By embracing our qualities and strengths, we not only find fulfillment and joy in our own lives but also have the opportunity to inspire and uplift others, making a positive and lasting difference in the world.

Connecting with others who share similar passions and goals can be a transformative experience on our journey to finding purpose. When we surround ourselves with like-minded individuals, we create a sense of belonging and community that nurtures our sense of purpose. Through these connections, we find support, inspiration, and a shared understanding of the challenges and triumphs we encounter along the way. Engaging with a community of individuals who share our passions and goals provides us with opportunities for collaboration, learning, and growth. We can exchange ideas, gain new perspectives, and find encouragement during times of doubt or uncertainty. Moreover, being part of a supportive community strengthens our commitment to our purpose and fuels our motivation to make a difference. Together, we can amplify our impact and create positive change, knowing that we are not alone in our pursuit of purpose. Connecting with others who share our passions and goals ignites a sense of collective purpose, reminding us that our individual journeys are part of a larger tapestry of meaningful action and shared aspirations.

Finding purpose in life often involves exploring different career paths and identifying how our unique skills and interests can be used to make a positive impact. It begins with self-reflection and gaining a deeper understanding of our strengths, values, and the causes or issues that resonate with us. By examining our skills and interests, we can start to envision how we can apply them in a way that aligns with our values and contributes to the greater good. It may involve considering different industries, roles, or even creating our own ventures. Exploring various career paths allows us to discover opportunities where we can combine our talents with our passion for creating positive change. It may take time and experimentation, but through this process, we can uncover fulfilling and purpose-driven work that not only utilizes our skills but also gives us a sense of meaning and fulfillment. By pursuing a career aligned with our values and making a positive impact, we can find purpose in our professional lives and contribute to a better world.

Engaging in volunteer work or community service can be a transformative experience that helps us discover our purpose and create a profound sense of connection to our community. By offering our time and skills to support causes we care about, we not only make a positive impact on the lives of others but also gain a deeper understanding of our own values and priorities. Volunteering exposes us to diverse perspectives, challenges us to step outside of our comfort zones, and allows us to witness firsthand the difference we can make in the lives of others. Through these experiences, we often discover new passions, talents, and areas where we can contribute meaningfully. Volunteering nurtures empathy, compassion, and a sense of collective responsibility, reminding us of the interconnectedness of our lives and the power we hold to effect change. It provides an opportunity to connect with like-minded individuals, forming bonds based on shared values and common goals. By engaging in volunteer work or community service, we embark on a journey of self-discovery, finding purpose in making a positive impact on the lives of others and forging deep connections within our communities.

Overcoming challenges and obstacles is an integral part of the journey towards discovering and fulfilling our purpose. It is through these trials that we develop resilience, inner strength, and a deeper understanding of ourselves. When faced with difficulties, we are presented with an opportunity to reassess our values, priorities, and aspirations. Challenges push us beyond our comfort zones and force us to confront our fears and limitations. As we navigate through setbacks and obstacles, we learn valuable lessons about perseverance, adaptability, and problem-solving. These experiences provide us with clarity and a greater sense of purpose as we realize what truly matters to us and what we are willing to fight for. The process of overcoming challenges instills in us a profound belief in our own abilities and strengthens our resolve to pursue our passions and make a meaningful impact. By embracing and surmounting these hurdles, we emerge with a renewed sense of purpose, armed with the knowledge that we have the capacity to overcome adversity and pursue our dreams with unwavering determination.

Living a purpose-driven life is a transformative journey that can uplift us from feelings of hopelessness and provide us with a clear sense of direction. When we align our actions and choices with our deepest values and aspirations, we tap into a wellspring of motivation and inspiration. Purpose infuses our daily lives with meaning and significance, giving us a compelling reason to get up each morning and make a difference. It ignites a fire within us, propelling us forward even in the face of challenges and setbacks. Living with purpose allows us to channel our energy towards endeavors that truly matter to us, whether it's making a positive impact in our communities, pursuing creative passions, or contributing to causes that align with our values. As we dedicate ourselves to a purpose greater than ourselves, we experience a profound sense of fulfillment and satisfaction. We feel a deep sense of connection to something larger, knowing that our actions are making a meaningful difference in the world. Living a purpose-driven life not only brings us joy and contentment but also helps us navigate the ups and downs of life with resilience and optimism. It provides us with a compass, guiding our choices and actions towards a path that aligns with our authentic selves. In doing so, we unlock our fullest potential and cultivate a profound sense of fulfillment that permeates every aspect of our existence.

We can embark on a profound journey of purpose by prioritizing our personal growth and continuous learning. When we commit to expanding our knowledge and developing new skills, we equip ourselves with powerful tools to contribute to the world in a meaningful way. Learning provides us with the opportunity to explore new perspectives, challenge our assumptions, and broaden our horizons. As we acquire wisdom and expertise, we gain the capacity to make a positive impact in our chosen areas of interest. Whether it's sharing our knowledge through teaching, mentoring others, or using our expertise to solve complex problems, our commitment to personal growth becomes the catalyst for meaningful contributions. By embracing lifelong learning, we not only enrich our own lives but also empower ourselves to create positive change in the world. Each new skill we acquire, each lesson we internalize, and each insight we gain becomes a building block in our purpose-driven journey. As we prioritize personal growth and learning, we discover our unique strengths and passions, and harness them to make a difference. Our newfound knowledge becomes a beacon that guides us towards impactful actions and projects, shaping our purpose and propelling us towards a life of significance.

Discovering purpose often necessitates venturing beyond the boundaries of our comfort zone and embracing risks to pursue our goals and passions. It requires a courageous leap into the unknown, where growth and transformation await. Stepping outside of our familiar routines and embracing the uncertainty that accompanies new experiences can be daunting, but it is within these moments of discomfort that we uncover hidden strengths, talents, and desires. By embracing risks, we challenge ourselves to break free from the limitations that confine us, allowing us to explore uncharted territories and tap into our fullest potential. Each risk taken is an opportunity for growth, learning, and self-discovery. It is through these bold endeavors that we uncover our true passions and forge a path aligned with our authentic selves. While the journey may be accompanied by fear and uncertainty, it is the willingness to take risks that propels us towards a life of purpose, fulfillment, and profound personal satisfaction.

In the midst of our busy lives, taking moments of stillness and reflection to meditate on our purpose can be transformative. By intentionally creating space for quiet contemplation, we allow our minds to settle, granting us the opportunity to gain clarity and perspective on our life's direction. Through meditation, we tap into our inner wisdom and intuition, connecting with the deeper layers of our being. In this sacred space of self-reflection, we can explore profound questions about our values, passions, and the impact we wish to make in the world. It is during these moments of stillness that the noise of external influences fades away, and the whispers of our true purpose can be heard. Through regular practice, we cultivate a heightened sense of self-awareness and a deep understanding of our core values, enabling us to align our actions with our purpose and live a more meaningful and fulfilling life.

In times of adversity, having a clear sense of purpose acts as a guiding light, illuminating the path ahead and fueling our determination. When faced with challenges, it can be all too easy to succumb to doubt, discouragement, or distraction. However, when we have a well-defined purpose, rooted in our values and aspirations, we find a reservoir of strength and resilience within us. Our purpose becomes the anchor that keeps us grounded and focused, reminding us of the greater meaning behind our endeavors. It serves as a constant source of motivation, igniting a fire within us to persist and overcome obstacles. With a clear sense of purpose, we are better equipped to navigate the stormy seas of adversity, staying committed to our goals, and ultimately emerging stronger on the other side.

Creating a vision board or visual representation of our purpose can be a powerful tool in manifesting our dreams and staying motivated along our journey. By gathering images, quotes, and symbols that resonate with our aspirations, we construct a tangible representation of our desired outcomes and the essence of our purpose. This visual reminder serves as a constant source of inspiration, fueling our motivation and reminding us of what we are working towards. Each time we look at our vision board, we reconnect with our deepest desires and reignite the passion that propels us forward. It becomes a visual roadmap that guides our actions and decisions, keeping us aligned with our purpose even when faced with challenges or distractions. The act of creating a vision board itself can be a transformative process, allowing us to clarify our intentions and visualize the life we wish to create. With our vision board as our compass, we navigate our journey with renewed focus and unwavering determination, knowing that every step we take brings us closer to realizing our purpose.

Finding purpose is not a passive endeavor; it requires us to actively engage in the process of self-discovery and intentional decision-making. It begins by reflecting on our values, passions, and the things that truly matter to us. By examining what brings us joy, fulfillment, and a sense of meaning, we can start to identify the activities, causes, or roles that resonate deeply with our core being. Once we have a clearer understanding of what matters most to us, we can then make intentional choices that align with our values and passions. This might involve pursuing a career that aligns with our interests, dedicating time to meaningful relationships, or engaging in activities that contribute to a cause we believe in. Finding purpose is an ongoing journey that requires continuous self-reflection and the willingness to adapt and grow along the way. By taking an active role in shaping our lives and making choices that align with our authentic selves, we can cultivate a sense of purpose that brings fulfillment, joy, and a deep sense of satisfaction.

Our unique identity is a tapestry woven from our experiences, strengths, passions, and values. Embracing who we are and recognizing the beauty in our individuality can be a powerful catalyst for finding purpose. When we accept and celebrate our unique identity, we tap into a wellspring of inspiration and strength. It allows us to explore and express our authentic selves without the constraints of societal expectations or comparisons to others. Our unique identity becomes a guiding light, illuminating the path to our purpose. It empowers us to leverage our strengths, pursue our passions, and make a meaningful impact that is aligned with our true selves. By embracing our uniqueness, we unlock the potential within us to contribute in ways that only we can, and to create a life filled with purpose, fulfillment, and a deep sense of self-acceptance.

In the busyness of life, it's easy to get caught up in the pursuit of future goals and overlook the beauty and significance of the present moment. However, embracing the present moment is essential for living a purpose-driven life. When we cultivate mindfulness and consciously engage with the here and now, we open ourselves up to the richness and depth of everyday experiences. We become aware of the small miracles and blessings that surround us, and we find joy in the simple moments of connection, laughter, and gratitude. Embracing the present moment allows us to fully immerse ourselves in the activities we love, to savor the beauty of nature, and to truly connect with the people who enrich our lives. It reminds us that life is not just about reaching future destinations but about finding meaning and purpose in each step of the journey. By embracing the present moment, we unlock the gateway to a purpose-driven life, where every day becomes an opportunity for growth, fulfillment, and the cultivation of a deep sense of gratitude and contentment.

Our purpose in life is not a static destination but a dynamic and evolving journey. As we navigate through different phases of life, our priorities, interests, and values may shift, and with them, our sense of purpose may also transform. Embracing this evolution is key to finding new opportunities for growth and fulfillment. Instead of clinging to a singular idea of purpose, we open ourselves up to the possibility of discovering new passions, exploring uncharted territories, and embracing change. We learn to listen to our inner voice and honor the callings that arise within us, even if they deviate from our previous path. Embracing the fluidity of our purpose allows us to adapt, learn, and grow, unlocking new dimensions of self-discovery and potential. By embracing the evolving nature of our purpose, we embark on a journey of continuous self-discovery, where each chapter brings fresh meaning, profound insights, and the limitless potential for growth and fulfillment.

19. Conclusion: The Importance of Personal Agency and Resilience in Overcoming Victim Chic.

In modern society, victimhood has taken on a significant cultural presence, with some individuals adopting the identity of a victim as a means to garner attention and sympathy. The allure of victimhood lies in the perceived power it can bestow upon someone, as society tends to respond with compassion and support when faced with stories of hardship and adversity. However, it is essential to recognize that while genuine victimhood exists and should be acknowledged, there is also a danger of embracing victimhood as a permanent state of being. The identification as a victim can create a cycle of self-perpetuating negativity, hindering personal growth and resilience. It is crucial to differentiate between acknowledging and healing from past wounds and perpetuating a victim mentality. By fostering a culture that encourages empowerment, self-responsibility, and resilience, we can challenge the narrative of victimhood and shift our focus towards personal growth, strength, and overcoming adversity.

While acknowledging the existence of genuine victims is crucial, the prevalence of victimhood culture can have adverse effects on personal growth and success. In a society that increasingly emphasizes victimhood as a means of gaining attention and validation, individuals may find themselves trapped in a mindset that perpetuates feelings of helplessness and dependence. The constant identification with victimhood can hinder individuals from taking ownership of their lives, pursuing opportunities, and overcoming challenges. It is important to strike a balance between acknowledging and addressing the injustices people face while also empowering individuals to rise above their circumstances and cultivate a sense of resilience and self-determination. By fostering a culture that encourages personal agency, accountability, and the pursuit of personal growth, we can create an environment where individuals can transcend the limitations of victimhood and strive for success and fulfillment.

A victim mentality, when deeply ingrained, can severely limit an individual's ability to take responsibility for their own life. By perceiving oneself as a perpetual victim, one may develop a sense of powerlessness, believing that external forces and circumstances have complete control over their destiny. This mindset can be detrimental, as it diminishes the individual's sense of agency and hinders their capacity to make proactive choices and take positive action. Instead of seeking solutions and actively working towards personal growth, those trapped in a victim mentality may become trapped in a cycle of blame, self-pity, and inaction. Overcoming a victim mentality requires a shift in mindset and a willingness to reclaim personal power by acknowledging one's role in shaping their own life and making choices that lead to growth and resilience. By cultivating a mindset of empowerment and personal accountability, individuals can break free from the limitations of victimhood and embrace their inherent ability to shape their own path.

Empathy, the ability to understand and share the feelings of others, is indeed a fundamental aspect of compassion. It allows us to connect with others, validate their experiences, and provide support in times of need. However, it is important to strike a balance between empathy and personal responsibility to prevent the perpetuation of victimhood culture. While it is crucial to acknowledge and validate the pain and challenges faced by others, it is equally important to encourage and empower individuals to take ownership of their lives and work towards solutions. Compassion that solely focuses on empathizing with victimhood without promoting personal responsibility can inadvertently reinforce a mindset of helplessness and dependency. By fostering empathy alongside the encouragement of personal agency, individuals can cultivate a more balanced approach that supports both understanding and accountability. This balanced perspective can contribute to the development of resilient individuals who are capable of overcoming challenges and pursuing personal growth while still extending compassion to those who are genuinely in need.

The attention economy, with its constant demand for captivating content, has played a significant role in the rise of victim chic within modern culture. Social media platforms and sensational news outlets often prioritize stories that evoke strong emotions and garner high levels of engagement. As a result, individuals may feel compelled to adopt a victim identity as a means to capture attention, sympathy, and validation from others. The allure of victim chic lies in the promise of instant recognition and support, albeit often short-lived. This phenomenon not only distorts the concept of victimhood but also creates a competitive atmosphere where individuals vie for the spotlight of victimhood, inadvertently undermining the experiences of those genuinely affected by adversity. The pervasive influence of the attention economy requires a critical awareness of the motivations behind claiming victim status, as well as a concerted effort to shift the cultural narrative towards empowerment, resilience, and the celebration of personal growth. By promoting a culture that values strength, self-reliance, and empathy for genuine hardships, we can foster a more balanced and constructive societal discourse that uplifts individuals rather than perpetuating a cycle of victimhood.

Intersectionality, a concept that recognizes the interconnected nature of social identities and systems of oppression, has a profound impact on shaping perceptions of victimhood. Factors such as race, gender, class, sexuality, and ability intersect to create unique experiences of marginalization and discrimination. These intersecting identities influence how individuals perceive and navigate their own victimhood. For example, a person's experience of victimhood may be shaped by their racial background, the discrimination they face based on their gender, and the economic barriers they encounter due to their class. Intersectionality highlights the importance of recognizing and addressing the multiple dimensions of oppression that individuals may face. It emphasizes the need to approach victimhood with an understanding of the complex ways in which power and privilege operate in society. By acknowledging the influence of intersectionality, we can work towards creating more inclusive and equitable spaces that validate the diverse experiences of victimhood and foster greater empathy and support for marginalized individuals.

Recognizing our own biases and privilege is a crucial step in breaking free from the victim mentality and cultivating personal agency and resilience. Biases, whether conscious or unconscious, can perpetuate a victim mindset by reinforcing negative narratives and limiting beliefs about ourselves and others. By acknowledging our biases, we can challenge them and open ourselves to new perspectives and possibilities. Similarly, recognizing our privilege allows us to understand the advantages and opportunities we may have had that others may not. This awareness enables us to approach our experiences with empathy and humility, fostering a mindset of growth and empowerment. It encourages us to take responsibility for our own lives and actions, rather than relying on external circumstances or attributing our struggles solely to victimhood. By actively confronting our biases and privilege, we can create a more inclusive and equitable world, while also nurturing our own personal development and resilience.

The media undoubtedly wields a significant influence in perpetuating victimhood culture, often amplifying stories and narratives that appeal to our emotions and reinforce a victim mentality. However, individuals possess the power to consume media mindfully and critically, thereby reclaiming control over their own perceptions and beliefs. By being vigilant about the sources and types of media we engage with, we can discern between genuine reporting of injustices and sensationalized narratives that fuel victimhood. Mindful media consumption involves seeking diverse perspectives, fact-checking information, and critically analyzing the underlying messages and agendas behind the content we encounter. By cultivating media literacy and maintaining an open mind, we can empower ourselves to make informed decisions about what narratives we choose to embrace, thereby mitigating the impact of victimhood culture and fostering a more balanced and empowered mindset.

Language is a powerful tool that shapes our thoughts, perceptions, and ultimately, our actions. It can either reinforce a victimhood mentality or promote empowerment and resilience. The words we choose to express ourselves and describe our experiences can have a profound impact on how we perceive ourselves and the world around us. By using language mindfully and intentionally, we can challenge the narratives of victimhood and instead focus on cultivating a language of empowerment. This involves reframing our experiences in a way that emphasizes personal agency, strength, and growth. It also means being mindful of the language we use when discussing others' experiences, avoiding labels or stereotypes that perpetuate victimhood and instead seeking to understand and support their journey towards empowerment. By harnessing the power of language, we can reshape our narratives and create a culture that fosters resilience, self-empowerment, and the belief in our ability to overcome challenges and thrive.

Overcoming victim chic and reclaiming personal agency requires a proactive and multifaceted approach. One strategy is setting boundaries to protect oneself from the allure of victimhood narratives. This involves recognizing when victim chic tendencies arise and consciously choosing to shift focus towards personal growth and empowerment. Cultivating resilience is another essential strategy, as it strengthens our ability to navigate adversity and bounce back from challenges. Building resilience involves developing coping mechanisms, seeking support from trusted individuals, and fostering a growth mindset. Practicing self-care is crucial in maintaining emotional well-being and preventing the allure of victimhood from taking hold. Engaging in activities that bring joy, practicing mindfulness, and prioritizing mental and physical health are vital aspects of self-care. Additionally, reframing trauma as an opportunity for growth can empower individuals to transform their experiences into sources of strength and wisdom. This involves embracing a mindset that views challenges as catalysts for personal development and using past traumas as fuel for resilience and self-discovery. By implementing these strategies, individuals can navigate away from victim chic and forge a path of self-empowerment, growth, and authentic fulfillment.

Forgiveness holds immense potential for healing and liberation, yet it is a deeply personal journey that varies for each individual. While forgiveness can be transformative, it is important to recognize that it is not always necessary or even possible in certain circumstances. Some individuals may find solace and closure through forgiveness, experiencing a profound sense of freedom by releasing resentment and letting go of the emotional burden tied to past trauma.

However, it is equally valid for others to prioritize their own well-being and choose alternative paths to healing, such as setting boundaries, seeking therapy, or focusing on self-care. Each person's healing journey is unique, and it is essential to honor one's own process and pace. Whether forgiveness is pursued or not, what matters most is finding a path towards healing and reclaiming personal power in a way that feels authentic and empowering for oneself.

Finding purpose and creating a meaningful life is a transformative process that empowers individuals to transcend the limitations of a victim mentality. When we identify our passions, values, and goals, we tap into a wellspring of inner strength and agency. Purpose gives us a guiding light, a reason to wake up each day with renewed enthusiasm and a sense of direction. It shifts our focus from past wounds to future possibilities, reminding us that we have the power to shape our own narrative. By actively engaging in activities aligned with our purpose, we take ownership of our lives and become active participants rather than passive recipients of circumstances. Purpose infuses our lives with meaning, serving as a driving force that propels us forward even in the face of adversity. It grants us the courage to step out of the victim's shadow, embracing our inherent potential and embracing the role of creator in our own life story. With purpose as our compass, we reclaim our power, cultivate resilience, and chart a course towards a life rich with meaning and fulfillment.

Personal agency and resilience are pivotal in breaking free from the clutches of victim chic. They empower individuals to rise above circumstances and reclaim control over their lives. Personal agency involves recognizing that we have the power to make choices and take action, even in the face of challenging circumstances. It is the belief that we are not helpless victims, but active participants in shaping our own destiny. Resilience, on the other hand, is the ability to bounce back from setbacks and adversity, to persevere in the face of challenges. It is the inner strength that allows us to adapt, grow, and thrive despite difficult circumstances. By cultivating personal agency and resilience, we break free from the victim narrative and embrace our innate capacity to overcome obstacles and create a life of purpose and fulfillment. We acknowledge that while there may be external factors that have influenced our journey, we ultimately have the power to shape our own destiny. By harnessing our agency and resilience, we dismantle victim chic and replace it with a mindset of empowerment and possibility.

It is crucial to acknowledge and honor the experiences of individuals who have endured genuine victimization, as their pain and suffering deserve recognition, support, and justice. Validating their experiences is an essential step towards healing and creating a more compassionate society. However, it is equally important to recognize the dangers of perpetuating victimhood culture, where individuals define their identity solely through victimization. This can inadvertently lead to a disempowered mindset that hinders personal growth and resilience. By striking a balance, we can create a space where we validate and support true victims while also encouraging empowerment, resilience, and a sense of personal agency. This involves fostering a culture that emphasizes individual strengths, resilience-building, and the pursuit of growth and transformation beyond the victim identity. It is a delicate balance that respects the experiences of victims while promoting a narrative of strength, resilience, and personal empowerment.

Mindfulness, self-reflection, and self-compassion are powerful tools that can help individuals recognize and overcome their own victim mentality. By cultivating mindfulness, individuals can develop a heightened awareness of their thoughts, emotions, and patterns of victimization. This awareness allows them to observe their victim mindset without judgment and with a compassionate understanding of its origins. Through self-reflection, individuals can delve deeper into their beliefs, experiences, and conditioning that contribute to their victim mentality. This process helps to uncover underlying fears, insecurities, and unprocessed emotions that may be keeping them stuck in a victim narrative. With self-compassion, individuals can nurture themselves with kindness and understanding, acknowledging the pain and challenges they have faced while also recognizing their innate strength and resilience. This combination of mindfulness, self-reflection, and self-compassion empowers individuals to challenge and transform their victim mentality, opening the door to personal growth, empowerment, and the creation of a more fulfilling and empowered life.

By taking responsibility for our own lives, we can break free from the cycle of victimhood and empower ourselves to create the life we want. This involves recognizing that we have the power to make choices and take action, even in the face of adversity. Instead of dwelling on past injustices or waiting for external circumstances to change, we acknowledge that our mindset, attitudes, and actions play a crucial role in shaping our reality. Taking responsibility means embracing accountability for our emotions, decisions, and outcomes, understanding that we have the capacity to change our circumstances through conscious effort and determination. It involves letting go of blame and shifting our focus towards personal growth, resilience, and self-empowerment. By owning our experiences and actively pursuing our goals and dreams, we reclaim our power and become active participants in creating a life of fulfillment, meaning, and success.

www.ingramcontent.com/pod-product-compliance
Lightning Source LLC
Chambersburg PA
CBHW061511250726
48657CB00005B/1793